Silent Aspirations

A NONVERBAL SON, HIS ART,
HIS MOTHER'S FAITH AND FAMILY'S BOND

SHAR BOEREMA

BEN BOEREMA,
ILLUSTRATOR

WESTBOW
PRESS®
A DIVISION OF THOMAS NELSON
& ZONDERVAN

THE HOLY BIBLE, NEW INTERNATIONAL VERSION®, NIV® Copyright © 1973, 1978,
1984, 2011 by Biblica, Inc.® Used by permission. All rights reserved worldwide.

Scripture taken from the New King James Version®. Copyright © 1982 by
Thomas Nelson. Used by permission. All rights reserved.

Scripture taken from the King James Version of the Bible.

This book is a work of non-fiction. Unless otherwise noted, the author and the publisher make
no explicit guarantees as to the accuracy of the information contained in this book and in
some cases, names of people and places have been altered to protect their privacy.

WestBow Press books may be ordered through booksellers or by contacting:

WestBow Press
A Division of Thomas Nelson & Zondervan
1663 Liberty Drive
Bloomington, IN 47403
www.westbowpress.com
1 (866) 928-1240

Because of the dynamic nature of the Internet, any web addresses or links contained in this book may have changed
since publication and may no longer be valid. The views expressed in this work are solely those of the author and do
not necessarily reflect the views of the publisher, and the publisher hereby disclaims any responsibility for them.

ISBN: 978-1-9736-4348-7 (sc)
ISBN: 978-1-9736-4347-0 (e)

Library of Congress Control Number: 2018912713

Print information available on the last page.

WestBow Press rev. date: 11/09/2018

THIS BOOK IS LOVINGLY DEDICATED TO:

"Ebomyne," my beloved husband and sharer in this beautiful tragedy. You have given up so many of my mental and emotional hours to the intensity of this book. Thank you for your encouragement, your contributions to this book, and for your love.

My passionate, hardworking, and beautiful daughters, Jen, Rachel, and Aubrey, for the loss of all my energy that went to your brother. Your written contributions in this book are my favorite parts! Your love for me and for Ben and your patience and encouragement throughout these years have often helped me start again.

The other man-child, son James. Thank you for sharing your great sense of humor, for being honorable and strong, and for being protective of your sisters and brother. I cherish your passion for the right, and admire your love and commitment to our country. Your kindness and thoughtfulness delight me, and your art is always fun!

Kelvin, our beloved son-in-law, your love for our daughter and your children is magnificent. Your hard work as a police officer and first responder defines you as a protector, and your love and respect for Ben makes me happy.

Anastasia, Kelvin Jr., and future grandchildren, I hope as you grow that your love for your uncle Ben stays strong and true, and that his life will inspire you to live yours well.

God … my Source, my Comforter, and my Inspiration.

And yes, Ben.
What a difference you make.
Your artwork finally has a platform!
You grew this work of heart.

TABLE OF CONTENTS

FOREWORD

"I have a tender and loving view of Ben that lingers, painting right over the hard years and challenging places." Shar Boerema writing about life with her son, Ben.

I have known the author of this book for 50 years. But actually, because of this book, I now have a deeper admiration and affection for the mother of Ben, the subject of this profoundly impactful book. When Shar asked me to read her manuscript, I already knew that she had a special needs son—now a six foot two-inch-tall 200-pound man. I knew that there were difficult moments over the last three plus decades. I knew that Ben lived in a special home for disabled adults. I knew that Shar was a great prayer warrior. But until this book, I didn't fully know why. Until this book, I didn't know the extent of her capacity for love, forgiveness and understanding. I now know the poetic side of her. I now know the gut wrenching sometimes sickening days she lived through as she, along with her beloved husband, Ed, raised a profoundly disabled son with an IQ in the twenties who is also bipolar and who suffers from severe attachment disorder.

The book drew me in over and over. It was as if I were an extra on a movie set watching, learning, feeling, observing. Imagine watching the laughter and the delight as Ben beats his brothers and sisters while bowling. Imagine the scene where Ben, the expert bowler, responding to the unusual sadness of his strong and able brother, throws gutter balls so his brother can win and be happy. Feel the emotion when non-verbal Ben draws the letter "B" into the palm of his mother's hand like Hellen Keller at the water pump. Picture a playground, and a disabled 10-year-old Ben playing at a park with the three and four year-olds who are in awe of him, his size, his laughter. Shar describes him at that moment as the "leading man."

At times, reading an episode (the chapters are written as stand-alone stories) filled my eyes with tears, not in pity, but in awe as I lived into the words so lovingly written about this "beautiful boy." A chapter in this book can whirl you around: One moment Ben is confused and violent and in another moment, exuberant and loving. Honestly stated, Shar writes about how Ben is strange and made their family strange. But there was no choice but to go on as a mother, father, brother or sister: To get up each day and play their parts, learning to trust God when there is no understanding.

I found this book to be like the Sunday sermon you remember and ponder all week. Shar teaches about forgiveness, love and grace with word pictures not easily forgotten. I have always wondered why Shar was so empathetic and why she seemed to understand the pain or the joy of her friends and family. It is in reading this book that I realized Ben's limitations expanded Shar's capacity. She had to become a vigilant observer of all things because her beloved child could cause chaos or panic at the drop of a hat. The chaos could be life-threatening, almost always terrifying. And at the very same time, she learned from her speechless son the gift of quiet and God's still small voice. Because of Ben she understood imperfection in a world that strives for perfection. She experienced the faithfulness of God through others in her faith and life community because they came alongside them for Ben to give respite care or a listening non-judgmental ear.

The philosophical questions in life are about opposites. How can two things be true? How are truths held in tension? In this book we hear from Ben's sisters who hold truth in tension. The difficult and frightening aspects of their brother also caused his siblings to be mature, empathetic, compassionate, and wise beyond their years. It shaped their vocations. Ben has enlarged the hearts and soul of his family. Ben has enlarged the hearts and soul of his church community. Ben has been a gift and also a beautiful tragedy.

The name of the book, *Silent Aspirations*, has a double meaning. It describes a medical condition as well as the potential inner life of Ben that we will never know from his own speech but get a glimpse of through his drawings interspersed throughout the book. By telling Ben's story, his deeply loyal and unconditionally loving mother gives voice to a son who has given her so much. Ben's influence has been profound. His disabilities, his lack of hypocrisy, his vulnerability resulted in him being a master teacher. And at the same time his disabilities, his need for 24-7 care, have caused anguish and suffering.

If you read one chapter, let it be chapter 24. Ben inexplicably attacks Shar in the church fellowship room. It is humiliating. She is unable to protect her son and herself. She journals later, "Can we just start over?" She concludes, on this side of heaven, the answer is, "No." But what Shar does give her readers is the opportunity to experience what she has come to understand as the deeper truth of the communion table, a table symbolizing the broken body and shed blood of her Savior, Jesus. Her experience with Ben allows her to know her Savior's anguish. She understands better, because of Ben, Christ's suffering on her behalf to give her and others a second chance—the ability to start over because of God's forgiveness and unfailing love. She writes, and we learn, "that forgiveness, of herself and Ben, is a huge part of loving."

Three final thoughts. First, God's tender mercies are revealed in this book over and over. Shar has an amazing talent to play the piano and to sing. There are many times when the words to familiar hymns rise from the stories. Great is thy faithfulness. The steadfast love of the Lord never ceases; his mercies never come to an end. How deep and wide the father's love; how vast beyond all measure. She writes, "I sing out my faith." Second, marriage can survive unexpected parenting responsibilities. The author writes, "Dealing with the mania Ben created made for a pressure cooker existence." I have read the statistics for how many marriages fail when there is a special needs child.

The blame and second guessing alone are crushing. And yet her partner for life, Ed, pledges to Shar in the midst of the mania, "You and I are in a war. I will never attack you. We need each other to survive."

Third, I was convicted that I had not been a very good friend over the last 40 years. I didn't take the time to ask questions. Deep, caring, I'd- like- to- know questions. Spurred by Shar's candor, I evaluate myself as a superficial journeyer through life with Shar. There was so much that I didn't know. But now, with this book, I have been able to catch up—to understand my friend in technicolor. I grew in empathy myself; weeping and laughing with her, even if belatedly. We've talked on the phone. She was so generous and kind at my confession. She said, "I didn't want many people to know because I thought they would reject Ben or be judgmental." Not an unrealistic fear. The book makes me ponder, "How can a Christian community come around all of us who have anguish or suffering in our lives that is hidden, that we are scared to share, because we fear judgment and rejection?" Because of Shar's courage and the revealing of her life with her beloved Ben, I am a changed person. For this I am grateful. I think you will be grateful too as you walk with Shar through the years of raising her beautiful boy, Ben.

Shirley V. Hoogstra, J.D.
President, Council for Christian Colleges and Universities

ENDORSEMENTS

The parade of those who suffer is long—very, very long—and the burdens each of them bears are heavy—very, very heavy. To enter into the sacred arena of their deep pain is an immensely important calling. But that calling begins with an awareness of pain and hurt, of distress and questions—in a word, of 'sadness'. How powerfully your book helped to remind of life's deep sadness. Thanks again for letting me read the manuscript. I was blest by it—deeply.

Dale Cooper
Chaplain Emeritus
Adjunct Faculty
Calvin College

For seven years, I worked very closely with Shar Boerema, encouraging ministry wives. Shar and her husband Ed have a severely disabled son. The two of them, along with their other children, have made an unusually beautiful team in raising their son and brother, Ben. Often Shar's life experiences with Ben helped people in our meetings who also had disabled children. I loved watching how Shar spent the needed time to listen to these women, offering empathy and being honest about the depth of her own pain. Shar's love and hope for Ben made it a transformative experience for the women. This is why I'm so pleased Shar has given herself to the arduous task of putting her life with Ben in print. Shar's faith and depth of love will delight any reader.

Gail MacDonald
(Wife of Gordon MacDonald
author, pastor)
Author
Cherished Friend

PREFACE

*Silent Aspiration*s is the story of our son, a man now, whose words are unspoken—silent—and whose mental capacities resemble a toddler's. It is also the name of the medical condition that threatens his life every day: silent aspiration. For me as his mother, though, it's probably his diagnosed mood disorders—the mental illness that threatened Ben's siblings, others, and his own safety—that is the most difficult of all to bear.

This book began with an overflowing folder entitled "Ben's drawings." It was full of pencil, ink, crayon, and marker scribbles, held in a metal file drawer crammed with reports, assessments, and legal documents, all about Ben. These squiggly doodles became familiar characters to me, revealing Ben's fabulous sense of humor and insights into his life that I would never otherwise have.

I wondered, of course, as he grew, "What are his aspirations? What do these drawings mean? Does he ever think about talking?" His thoughts and aspirations would probably be lost except for this extraordinary, artistic look into his life. Each sketch replaces sacred conversations we never had, and reminds me of the facts, emotions, or memories we made. I began to pull together my own faith journey, using his drawings to give definition to the privileged, turbulent, funny, and deeply painful years as his parent.

That file of drawings may be more important to me than the ones swelling with doctors' test results, or teachers' agonizing attempts to find new ways to avoid the words "no change." It reveals more about him than the scores of psychologists' behavioral plans, carefully listing strategies for *dealing with*, *avoiding*, or *recovering from* Ben's behaviors.

We all wrestle with imperfection and disappointments. But, it doesn't take much research to find numbers as high as 1 in 25 Americans dealing with severe mental disorders. Many people, irrespective of intelligence quotient, deal with perplexing, sometimes devastating mood disorders. I believe this work is poignantly validating to those, like Ben, who are one of those persons or who feel ostracized. It is also important to the many who love those Bens. After reading these pages, I hope my readers will better understand the way those behaviors impact our families and our communities. I also hope we will find new ways to traverse this minefield.

My not-so-silent aspiration is to honor God by sharing the gift of Ben's life, his humor, his joy, his abilities, his idiosyncrasies, and his sufferings. My prayer is that I have found the right words to describe this complex person, and to give a shout-out to the people in his life. My aspiration is to shine a bold beacon on the Bens in our world, while allowing my readers to laugh out loud at his sparkling humor and resilience. I pray our story will inspire others to mine deep for the beauty often found in the middle of a tragedy.

ACKNOWLEDGMENTS

Love and forever thanks to all the saints in Ben's life—and mine—who keep "marching in." Way too many to list here! You are amazing people!

Rev. Dale Cooper, though I've long admired your faith and reputation, we first met through my CDs and your appreciation for the Psalms, as I arranged and sang them. Your gift of time encouraged me when I was truly in complete despair. You continued that encouragement with each uplifting word you wrote in the following years. You are the first person I trusted with Ben's story, and you got the message immediately. Your encouragement to me to "keep singing" and to share this story gave me the courage I needed. Your endorsement—priceless!

Ben's peeps: You know who you are: aides, house supervisors and staff, clinical support staff, caseworkers, teachers, bus drivers, families of his peers: Beautiful, beautiful people. You are so loved!

Gail MacDonald, beloved friend and mentor for so many years, your life and books first fed my spirit and my writer's bug. My delightful friend, thank you for every hour you spend responding so completely and quickly to my emails and texts, and to my peeps. You lift me up! Your endorsement is cherished.

Deb Walburg, you are an amazing encourager! Here it is! Girlfriend, lifetime connector, and best owner/lender/groomer of our beloved collie, Cruiser! Your Jen and our Ben would have made a great couple in life.

To my gentle-spirited daughter Jen, who invited me to share years of walks under and around the blossoming trees during Calvin College's Festival of Faith and Writing—thank you! Those conferences grew me up into the world of words that you have always loved. And yes, we share in this *beautiful tragedy*.

My darling sisters Janet, Judy, Karen, Carrie, Ruth, Deb, and Anita Zuidema (another WestBow Press author: *She Walks in Beauty and Endless Light*); your love, sisters, sustained me, and every moment we spend together is pure gift!

Eric Toth, design leader at Haworth and friend, your personal hours scanning and working Ben's drawings into the proper format for *Silent Aspirations* was an enormous gift; thank you.

To the MOKA Organization and all its supporters: your care and provision for Ben have made my life and this book possible. I hope I adequately describe what a difference you make in people's lives every day.

To H. B. London Jr. (1936-October, 2018), Judy Devries, Verdell Davis Krisher, and Gail MacDonald, who, along with Focus on the Family, welcomed me to their team for seven years: the breakout sessions for women dealing with special-needs family members cemented this vision.

And to my class of '74 high school girlfriends (including Shirley, who graciously agreed to write the foreword to this book): your love helped me survive, and your lives—lived so well—helped me write about mine.

A resounding, relieved, appreciative thank you to the editors and staff at West Bow Press that helped me navigate the scary self-publishing world! Thank you for moving my son, Ben, from my laptop to the marketplace where people will finally see Ben's gifts and really get to know him and his beautiful heart! I hope this book will find its way to many who need encouragement.

INTRODUCTION

Since we have always lived in West Michigan, our kids grew up with the dunes and beaches as their summer playground. Most often our destination was the White Lake channel, where we lived for almost twenty years. We enjoyed a few holiday breakfasts at one of its lonely picnic tables next to the path, under the poplars. That was, until our teenagers got too embarrassed by the publicity of it all!

Watching sailboats, yachts, speedboats, and fishing boats coming in from Lake Michigan, happy boaters waving to us as they motored into the big lake, meant summer for us. It was an excellent spot for watching people fish at the metal railing or out on the pier, greeting community friends, or watching people walk around the White River Lighthouse on the other side of the channel.

Sometimes our kids climbed the dune, running into the lake from there. My husband reminded me why people run down dunes: you end up taking considerably longer strides than you ever could just running! You cannot walk down a dune—you have to run or slide—holding your body erect, with arms flailing to keep from somersaulting forward. Sand cushions your feet with each accelerated step, aiding the downward gravitational pull. The thrill of running straight into Lake Michigan is very close to the feeling one gets on the scary descent of a towering roller coaster.

Ben, on the other hand, walked down the cement sidewalk, eager to get to the sand. He waited for help navigating the bleached boulders on the edge, usually working his way to a spot close to the water. Then, slowly he would land on both knees, backside to the water, on partially wet sand. With his hands, a shovel, a bucket, or a cup—anything we remembered to bring or could repurpose from leftover plastic containers—he started digging.

He could sit for hours, watching bugs or methodically creating a huge hole while alternately releasing dripping wet sand through his fingers. Occasionally, he screeched when a noisy seagull flew in too close, warning it with a swipe of his hand. At the same time, he beckoned with his index finger to children wondering what he was doing. Children and their parents were obviously puzzled by the strange squeals and squawks coming from that grown boy.

One has to shield their eyes from the brilliance of a million diamonds dancing over Lake Michigan when staring out over its beautiful expanse. But calm usually seeped into the busy crevices of my mind as warm sand worked its magic between my toes, inviting me to sit or lie down.

Chatter—even the chatter of my family—was hushed by the lazy, rhythmic waves lapping the shore. I would be struck mute by the frequent calls of seagulls, by lovers old and young walking hand in hand. Children's busy conversations always reminded me how easily words come to most people.

Ben typically made a trip into the water at least once, if only to wash off the sand before we left. Departure usually came with great moaning and complaints. If the lake was placid, he would venture into it earlier on. Sometimes we had to coach him in, squealing at the cold. The waves made him giggle and gasp. We helped him out, drying his long legs, putting his tennis shoes back on. Reaching for our help, he squawked and waved goodbye to the curious children.

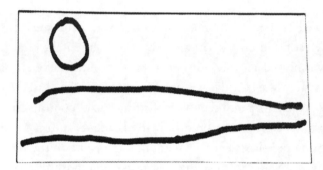

This simple drawing, like the other sketches you'll discover in this book, reminds me of all I have to learn from Ben. Using two of the few shapes he perfected—the circle and the line—he calls me to be still, to listen to the waves, to dig my toes in the sand, and to feel the movement of the water. He calls me to simply be aware of God all around me.

Just by the way he drew these three lines, I am reminded how God uses the praise of "children and infants … to silence the foe and the avenger." Psalm 8:2(NIV) Ben's voice remains, because of those simple lines. The waves strip away all the world's babble.

CHAPTER 1

Kangaroo Class

One of the most important I would ever attend!

Creaking swings, children's laughter, and mothers' giddy conversations sparkled over the airwaves like the sunshine spilling through the tall oaks that day. Braking to park on the twig-filled gravel, I tried to hold back the energy of my lanky nine-year-old.

"Wait a minute, Ben! We have to loosen your seat belt!" I warned while double-checking the zipper and snap on his jeans.

"Yaaah." He grinned, his eyes glazing over at the sight of the giant slide.

Hoping to divert him, I pointed to the swings. "Shall I push you, Ben? Look!"

"Uh-uh." He shook his head.

"No? Okay. Be careful! Momma's going to sit right here with my book," I lied to myself.

Strollers and bikes covered the lawn. We had moved from this community about a year before. Ben enthusiastically drank in the sights and memories of this special place as he trudged forward. Happy babies invited his look, while hot dogs sizzled on a grill somewhere, reminding us all that we were here to play.

With arms swinging, Ben smiled at everyone. He headed straight for the steep spiral slide. His left foot curved in and dragged a little, but he purposefully sloughed through the sand, leaves, and bark, his eyes trained on the goal.

Active boys his age were into play that was well beyond him. He had worked hard learning things other children acquired naturally, but his brain was still only capable of two-year-old thoughts and accomplishments. His speech capability lingered between six months and a year.

I noticed some boys around his age gathering near him. He may have said "Hahee," or touched one of the boys in greeting. As they fixed their stares on Ben, poking one another in superiority, I felt nauseated. For a slight moment, pain and confusion shimmered in Ben's beautiful blue eyes. Holding his face in my hands, I reminded him of Daddy's consistent encouragement: "You're the best, Ben!"

Undaunted, Ben pulled away, wobbling toward the oversize red play equipment.

"This is *your* day, buddy! Go for it!" I cheered, more positively than I felt.

A little tipsy, he gripped the handrails. Slowly, he began his climbing procedure on the metal steps: right foot up first, followed by the weaker left. We had practiced three or four times in different parks, and I knew I'd have to let him solo it sooner or later. Ben had decided on sooner.

Raucous boys and girls pressed in, yelling, "Hurry up, slowpoke!"

Right foot up, left foot up, right. Without any apology, Ben frequently stopped to wave at them, repeating "Hi!" and hitting at them when they got too close.

Active, healthy boys elbowed and jostled, propelling their bodies up two steps at a time. I whispered, "Please, God! Help him hold on!"

Ben grinned down at me and, in his high, shrill voice, yelled, "Hahee!" Then, as if perched on the top step of a jet he was about to pilot, he waved, hand straight out and flat, with the tips of his fingers bending in his typical baby's wave.

"Hold on … Wow!" I smiled hesitantly at my gentle son. "Remember how to sit now, Ben!" I held my breath, the heavy thumping in my chest drowning any other thoughts or sounds as he maneuvered fifteen feet in the air, precariously situating himself at the top. "Get your feet out straight!"

"Yeah?" he half screamed as he disappeared sideways, his hysterical giggle now swallowed by bumps at every bend—all the way down. His adversaries quickly followed, jumping off behind him short of the end, glaring, and running off. Stooping to the dirt, I helped Ben to his feet, brushed away his tears, and clapped.

He rubbed his arm. "Muhma," he pouted.

"Yes, Momma saw you! You'll be fine, big guy. *Way to go*, Ben! You did it all by yourself!" With an exaggerated sweep, I lifted my hand for a high five, bringing back his smile. I beamed as he rambled away, seemingly without a second thought about his enormous triumph.

Nearby, younger children were hopping up and down on what looked like two teeter-totters at right angles to each other, pivoting on a base in the center. The name, Kangaroo, was faded and worn. With a loud cry and sort of an "oh-oh" screech, Ben bolted toward a curly-headed little girl who had erupted in weeping, perched on one of the seats. I got there just as he gently leaned over to hug her, abruptly halting her cries. Before I could stop him, he planted a kiss on her cheek.

She was mesmerized by her gentle hero. Her eyes followed Ben as he lumbered toward the merry-go-round. Glancing back, he made faces and bellowed out short, shrill syllables for her to copy. He wiggled his tongue at her in a taunting dare, then flapped his hands by his ears.

In a trance, she followed, starting to experiment with her tongue. The sun shone through the frizzled ends of her reddish-blonde hair. Her pudgy kindergarten arms offered a baby-size push to Ben as he struggled onto the metal circle.

Slowly, I twirled the rotating platform for them and other curious children climbing aboard, drawn to the boy like a magnet. "Hi! His name is Ben. What's yours?" I queried.

"Ben, look at me! Ben! Ben! Watch me, Ben!" the others squawked, vying for his attention.

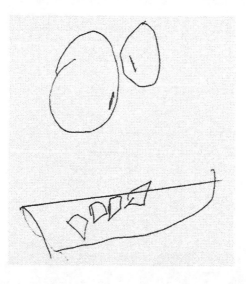

Starting to relax, I introduced them to one another, assuring them that sticking out one's tongue was okay in the way Ben was doing it: "He's playing with you!" They wagged theirs too, mimicking his silly sounds. Shrieking, laughing, acting like two-year-olds, they came up with some sounds of their own as they laughed and played without embarrassment.

I backed up then, fascinated by this leading man, enjoying his role with new friends. Settling into a low-hanging swing with the unopened book on my lap, I knew that the class I'd just experienced could be one of the most important I would ever attend.

I labored over the next two-plus decades, reenacting sounds and syllables. I prayed and searched for exact words and word pictures that would somehow capture the strength and character of Ben—once a wordless boy, now a man I am so privileged to call my son.

CHAPTER 2

Beautiful Tragedy

The worry, but never the belief

"Who wants to pray?" Ben's daddy would often ask at the table.

Ben's hand flew up frequently. Pulling his tightly folded hands up to his dimpled face, he would lower his head, eyes peeking between the almost-closed lids.

"Who wants to pray for Ben?" was the next question.

"I do!" I would quickly respond. "Lord, Ben wants to say he loves You. He loves us too."

"Yah," drawled Ben.

"Ben wants to thank you for this great day and good food."

"Yah."

"And Lord, we want to say thank you too … for Ben."

"Meh!" he would bark, reaching for his spoon.

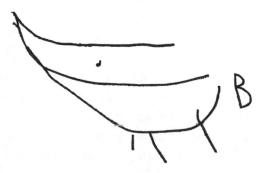

With his signature approving it,
I think we can consider this a self-portrait.
I've called it *The Big Hungry Mouth!*

Many, many people have asked what Ben's diagnosis is. Cerebral palsy? Fragile X? Autism? No. Not any of them. Ben looked physically perfect, so Down syndrome was never assumed. For the first year and more, we didn't notice many of the signs that were obvious to others, because we were so delighted with our ever-smiling, stocky, blond-haired baby boy.

What we could not ignore were the sleepless nights: one after another, with four to five broken hours of sleep on any given night. The pediatrician suggested letting Ben cry. We tried that for eleven nights straight one time, with no resolution.

No cloth was big enough to handle Ben's upchucks. The gastroesophageal reflux problem was huge. Nothing seemed to help—soy milk, goats' milk, expensive formulas. The pediatrician had no solutions.

As Ben approached, then passed his first birthday, I tried to tell the doctor about Ben's delays in movement and speech. I asked about home therapy. Repeatedly, he dismissed any worries, implying I was just a "nervous mom."

Finally, long after Ben's first birthday, Ben's aunt Janet—a registered nurse—dared to approach us with gentle suggestions based on her observations. She gave us the name of a highly respected pediatric specialist. That visit began the critical move to a new pediatrician—a very detailed and caring doctor, Charlotte Worpel. She sent us directly to a neurosurgeon, wanting to rule out the possibility of a brain tumor.

We prayed there would be no tumors, of course, and prayed that God would heal Ben. But, somewhere in the backs of our minds, we began to believe that a tumor might be *the problem*. Maybe Ben's slow development—taking his first steps at twenty-one months, talking in only two syllables, sleeping so little, eating insatiably, and flaring into horrible tempers—could all be explained by the existence of a tumor. We even hoped there was something that *could* be surgically removed to fix all those problems.

Ed and I focused on praying for good news. We prayed before walking into the neurosurgeon's office for the results. But we were both shocked by his report.

We had focused our prayer on "God, heal that tumor" and "thank you, God, for healing Ben." And we thanked him for the child we were expecting. I remember walking, hand in hand and smiling, toward the doctor's office that February day, feeling very confident that God had probably already healed Ben. We held to that statement of belief—that hope—for a long time afterward.

The young specialist held the MRI report in his hand as we sat across from him at his cluttered desk. He shook his head thoughtfully, leaning back a little in his chair. Slowly, he explained that there was no sign of a tumor or anything else visible. The developmental delays and behaviors were probably signs of mental impairment (now more commonly called "intellectual disability" or "developmental delays"). "There's nothing more we can do."

Thinking there might be a specialist who would have other solutions, we asked, "What should we do next?"

Quietly, he suggested we talk with the people at Ottawa Area Center in Allendale, Michigan. I knew the place he was talking about, but my only knowledge of it was as a building where people who were disabled went. I had no terminology for "those" people at that point. Fear gripped my heart. *NO! Not my beautiful son! Not our handsome, dimpled blond joy!*

I had had the worry, but never the belief. I wanted to run, to fight it with everything in me. That news did send me to the hospital, repeatedly, with early labor. Our beautiful, raven-haired Rachel—Little Lamb, as we called her—was born just twenty-three days after Ben's second birthday.

We first hoped that the "no tumor" diagnosis meant Ben was healed. It was another form of denial, stemming back to Ben's earliest months. A specialist, some years later, surmised that Ben's developmental delays pointed to a "global encephalopathy," meaning everything in Ben's brain was affected by whatever it was that caused the delays in the first place. Specialists believe a virus attacked his cerebral matter during its critical development at two months in utero. Years later, more extensive tests revealed nothing genetically alarming. The typical description now is "global developmental delays."

We had no way of knowing what the ramifications of that diagnosis were for us. That was probably good. I'm honestly grateful we had those first two years of ignorance, just enjoying Ben for who he was. We did not compare him to our firstborn—his older sister Jenny, to whom reading, talking, and learning came early and so naturally. His daddy had visions of football and cars for his firstborn son. Ben was just himself.

We are grateful for Michigan's responsiveness to Ben's needs. Proactive treatment is not available in every state. I know there are parents who are left to find their own solutions—regardless of their child's diagnosis or concerns—sometimes they are only offered regular public school education. We are eternally grateful to the parents and professionals who built Ottawa Area Center, in Ottawa county, and Wesley School in Muskegon, long before we needed them. According to disabilityscoop. com, Michigan is still listed among the top ten states for the proactive treatment of people with developmental delays.

Things started moving very quickly after our visit to Ottawa Area Center. Ben's plan called for an occupational therapist (Carol) to begin visits immediately, several times each week. Lugging in a case full of tools each time, she brought exercises and activities for Ben's two-year-old tongue, ideas to encourage his swallowing, and toys and gadgets to develop his fine motor skills. And food—food has always been a strong incentive for Ben!

I assumed Carol's goal was to help Ben learn to talk, but I soon realized that speech was only part of his disability. He wasn't chewing normally either. Carol stressed how many connections have to take place in the brain for a person to chew and swallow safely and correctly.

My other children, and now Jen's children, surprise and delight me with how bright a healthy mind is. There is such a stark difference in those critical early learning years when developmental delays are at work.

Ben often coughed or choked when eating. We thought he was wolfing down food and drink too fast. We were wrong. Even with all the therapists and physicians who worked with Ben over the following years, it wasn't until we asked for a swallowing test that he was diagnosed with silent aspiration, many years later. As I understand it, silent aspiration is defined as a liquid or even solid food getting into the trachea below the vocal cords, without noticeable signs like coughing, choking, reddened face, or change in respiration. I've written about Ben's near-fatal stint with pneumonia (a result of silent aspiration) in chapter twenty-one.

Jenny, just twenty-two months Ben's senior, watched Carol intently. Jenny was barely four years old herself. I grieved the attention lost to her and lavished on Ben. I knew Jen would have loved to play with those brightly colored toys, but it also suited her curiosity and motherly instincts of observation. She became adept beyond her years: picking up Ben's dropped toys, helping Carol, and soothing Ben's anxiety when she noticed tears of exasperation starting to swell.

Jen and I have enjoyed sharing several delightful conventions together, called Festivals of Faith and Writing, at Calvin College, in Grand Rapids, Michigan. She first suggested *A Beautiful Tragedy* as the name for this book on the way home from one of those inspiring weekends together. Ben's intellectual losses are catastrophic. We never imagined how our children's lives, our faith, and Ben's courage would be tested through those years. But we also never conceived of the beauty God would develop in Ben's life and ours, in the midst of such a tragedy.

The comfort of Jenny—that darling, blond-haired four-year-old with her bright mind— brightened the early days of Ben's diagnosis. We live near Jen and her husband, Kelvin, now. They have two darling children (Ana and Kelvin Jr.) who we enjoy so much! Jen is a thoughtful, fun mom and daughter, and a beautifully compassionate woman, working with several nonprofit organizations, as a virtual administrative assistant.

The beautiful baby born just after we learned Ben's diagnosis—Rachel—remains a delightful comfort to me even today. The creaking of our heirloom rocking chair accompanied the lullaby she most heard from me during her first year. I sang and hummed this old chorus, willing myself to believe that:

> Jesus never fails. Jesus never fails.
> Heav'n and earth might pass away, but
> Jesus. Never. Fails.

CHAPTER 3

Owed to Benjamin

A child of our love … born like the others;
Yet what an impact you've made on our lives!
Your smile captures hearts. You radiate joy.
You speak with your smile, your kisses, your hugs.
No language is needed. You love with your eyes.

You've been appointed to an extraordinary task:
To open our eyes to the world of the meek,
To lift us beyond intelligence or fame,

There we see Jesus, though hidden to most,
In the eyes of the helpless and weak.

Progress is slow when we measure by "norms."
Achievements are measured best by the heart.
We must learn from the silence,
Speak with our smiles, our kisses, our hugs.
No language is needed when we love with our eyes.

I wrote this poem when Ben was still young. Ben has never learned the value of money, but the drawing has always reminded me of a bundle of dollar bills and coins; a reminder of how much we owe Ben and all our children for the gifts they've given that no money in the world could buy!

CHAPTER 4

Dangerous Denial

Something about Ben's attitude changed

That poem describes the best of Ben. His personality, without the bipolar mania, would always choose fun and laughter. The prankster in him comes through in this grown-up picture with his younger sister Rachel, after they had just played his favorite game: peekaboo around the maple tree. It's the way we wish things were all the time.

Most of the time, Ben was a happy child. Nights were hard right from the beginning, but we seemed to wake up each day with the belief that the next night would be better. A nap or an eight-hour night would come soon. It just never happened. Our excuses for his severe or persistent behaviors were real. Sometimes that denial affected the other children.

I had written most of this book but still wanted to leave out some incidents that happened long ago between Ben and his siblings. Then I thought, *Why* not *just tell what happened?* I'm sure I still feel some guilt for "letting" these things happen, for not being more careful or even aware. I became defensive of Ben, always conscious of protecting his reputation.

I didn't have any specific reason to worry about Ben with Rachel, but he was a tall, very clumsy, unbalanced, energetic toddler, just twenty-five months older than her. This particular day is murky and gray in my memory. I think it was fall, a rainy day that marked the beginning of a chilling fear I tried to stuff down for many years. I was excited to drop off four-year-old Jenny for some play time with new friends at their house.

I left Rachel in her car seat as I took Jen into the house. She might have been six months old. Ben was, I think, buckled into the backseat. Car seats were brand-new, so I probably only had one for Rachel, as the baby. I left them together because I planned to come right back. They were both quiet and happy. (Famous last words!)

I'll never forget stepping out of the house moments later, to the horrible, breathless screams of our baby. Her terrified little face was covered in fresh streaks of blood. At first, I didn't associate it with Ben. He was upset, but I didn't know why. I didn't know if she'd started crying and he didn't know what to do, or if something else had happened.

Here's the thing: I don't believe I even *thought* of the possibility that he could attack her. I didn't believe any child would do that to another! I took them both into our friend's house, cleaned baby Rachel's face, and comforted her… and Ben. The incident troubled me, but I didn't know what it meant.

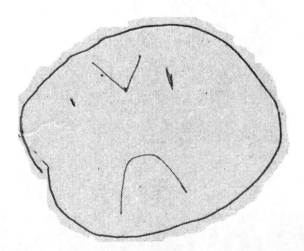

I now believe that was one of the first manifestations of Ben's mental illness, which would raise its ugly head throughout the following years periodically and forcefully, but would not be entirely diagnosed until sixteen years later.

Now there are psychiatrists and group sessions for siblings of children with developmental delays. At that time there were none, or at least none I knew about. I wish we had knocked down some doors to find or ask for those resources.

Ben was ten years old when Aubrey was born and twelve when James arrived. They were the subjects of mysterious incidents too. A dislocated shoulder for infant Aubrey could only be explained by an encounter with her brother Ben. We also have a video of Ben holding and kissing four-month-old James. Studying it objectively, I realized I quickly stopped the recording when something about Ben's attitude changed, and I promptly rescued James from Ben's tightening arms.

A few years later, on the farm, we found the children's pet bunny, Annie, was killed. Multiple kittens also were found dead after we had allowed Ben to hold them.

Ben never developed the knowledge and restraint of a child older than two. But his physical strength did develop. For those reasons and probably some I don't know about, James and Aubrey grew up more scared than we knew of their big brother.

Rachel never seemed to fear Ben. At least she never *showed* him her fear. Both she and Jen were devoted to him. Their lives were formed in many ways by him. Most of the time, that led to giggles and adventures. I've included chapters written by his sisters that better describe their complicated and tragically beautiful relationship. But this story is the beginning of things that would increasingly alienate Ben from society, sometimes from family, and definitely from his peers.

Denial can be a great thing! It allows one to live fully and not imagine or fear the worst. It allows one to thoroughly enjoy the moment. Denial was not a choice any longer when it came to Jen's children—our grandchildren and Ben's niece and nephew. We all agreed that Ben would not be allowed to touch them in their first year or so. The risk was too high for one awful, impulsive move. Though I was the one most likely to fail in that commitment, we saw it through. Caution ruled then so that they could later have a loving, trusting relationship with their uncle Ben.

Slowly the precautions were relaxed a little. They now have a wonderful time playing together—not without careful monitoring, but they have the opportunity to positively express their love and joy for one another.

Little Ana, at four years old, is very much like her momma and her aunt Rachel were. She has never been afraid of Ben, only wanting to be loving and naturally close to him, though Ben tested that really for the first time, while we were taking family pictures in July of 2018. She has a better understanding of why we're cautious, but she is still innocent of the worst of the bipolar monster. Thankfully, she was again playing lovingly with him the next few times they were together. (Always with our vigilant observance.)

One beautiful moment is etched in my mind from Christmas, 2017. She couldn't wait to see him and ran into our house, screaming "Ben!" She didn't stop to hug me but jumped into his lap, cuddling on his shoulder as he gently embraced her. They enjoyed the sheer joy of being reunited for a full minute with me hovering nearby—cautiously monitoring, ready to intervene if necessary. I wish I'd grabbed the camera instead!

Then two-year-old Vinny did the same thing when he walked into our home at Easter. His step quickened as he headed directly to the kitchen to cuddle up to Ben. Such a gift!

CHAPTER 5

Antennae Man and Timid Girl

Acknowledging loss, embracing hope, and setting a new course.

"Hahee!" Ben belted out as he charged across our church sanctuary. We had to work at restraining him or just clumsily bolt with him, excusing ourselves through the milling crowd of two thousand people as he headed toward someone he couldn't wait to greet.

This character shows an antennae sticking right out of the face, like hospitality and warmth oozing from his face. Ben never tired of greeting his friends or little strangers, always with a passion most of us reserve for loved ones we haven't seen in a year! He used that passion every Sunday and still reacts that way, even if we've just recently seen him. It's taken us and all of Ben's teachers and aides *years* to teach Ben to shake hands instead of hug. His preferred greeting is still a "holy" kiss. This is the young Ben we remember.

Ben seems to have come specially equipped with spiritual antennae, sometimes called *feelers*, enabling him to zero right in on the feelings of the people around him. Intuitively, he knows who desperately needs his hug. Sometimes all it takes is his monosyllabic, exuberant greeting to bring transformation to a sad face.

It looks like this character might have two sets of eyes. That fits Ben too. His beautiful, sparkly eyes are able to speak friendship and love from across a roomful of people. He seems to have a Holy Spirit way of knowing who needs a special touch. So often we have heard, "I *needed* Ben today!"

How amazing! Ben is a person whose speech consists of a few inarticulate, high- and low-pitched syllables, with an intelligent quotient in the low twenties. Yet he can instinctively minister to the pain or need in someone else's life. God knew (*foreknew*, to use a rare term) and equipped him, and I believe Ben delights God as he uses that gift.

"Let your life be a sermon. If necessary, use words." That familiar phrase has often resonated with us as we've watched Ben preach his sermons. Yes, sometimes his instruction has come through horrible behaviors, but usually it comes through happy, unexpected moments of grace and loving.

After one candlelight Christmas Eve service, many years ago, Ben escaped our firm handhold and ran to give a big hug to a friend whom he hadn't seen in several months. Doug came to me later with tears in his eyes, saying, "I needed Ben today!" Doug went on to relay that after spending many months fighting in Iraq, his son arrived home in time for Christmas—only to learn that two of his buddies had lost their lives just after he left. What does Ben know of war? Yet his antennae had *felt* the heaviness and ministered love and healing that Christmas Eve.

Shortly after Ben's disabilities were diagnosed, Ed and I began to plead with God for his complete healing. Many friends joined us for days devoted to prayer and fasting. Some still faithfully pray.

Ben was not healed in the way we asked. But, as we listen and learn, God has shown us a beautiful, possibly higher path for Ben.

It is my joy to use this book to encourage others to recognize the God-given antennae that belong to people with developmental, behavioral, physical, and mental health disorders. They are uniquely designed for their world, especially for those of us who need them.

That is how I ended this chapter originally. My perspective could possibly be seen as just a tad over spiritualized, yes? I really believe it, and it's all true. But, I purposefully left out many of Ben's really disruptive behaviors to achieve my point.

Jen has the unique perspective as Ben's only "big" sister (older, but smaller, for sure). She is quieter than Ben, temperamentally. But, as you will see, she has pretty good antennae of her own!

She is a great writer, and for quite a few years wrote a blog[1] called "Little tribe of Benjamin" (taken from Psalm 68:27a(NIV), a verse we claimed as special for our Ben: "There's the little tribe of Benjamin, leading them…"

She compares our Benjamin with the Benjamin from the Old Testament saying, "The biblical story of another [Benjamin's birth] seems to fit our attitude toward him: acknowledging loss, embracing hope, and setting a new course because of a painful experience."

This, then, is from her description on the blog's first page: "Although we have grieved often over the pain of "imperfection" in Ben's life, he is not defined by sorrow. We can't imagine our lives without him! It would be like losing our right hand. And like the little Jewish tribe of Benjamin, he leads us all the time. In courage, trust, patience, joy, love, and hope, Ben sets the example.

Of course, he also leads the way in creating chaos and causing trouble!

When you love someone with special needs, it's gonna hurt, and it's gonna be complicated. But that love is also a source of deep joy and uncommon grace. This site is a place to explore the unique beauty of "Benjamites" and remind us of the way God redeems the bleak and offers hope."

If you read between the lines of the following April, 2010 post[2], "Church—Siblings with Special Needs", you won't have to look far to see the loneliness of her childhood. Don't miss it! Being a sibling of a special-needs person can be *very* lonely at times.

From Jen's April 2010 blog
"Church—Siblings with Special Needs"

I'm the oldest but Ben was born before I was two, so I don't have any memories of our family without him. I don't have many memories before five or six, actually, which is probably normal. I do remember a lot from our time at church, though… Ben has always had severe separation anxiety, so he did better in Sunday school if he was with me or Rachel. Even then, I don't think he made it through an entire morning very often without a behavioral problem that required my parents to be called from the service. The whole situation was hard. Because Ben was with me, I was different.

We moved to a new church when I was about five and I was a shy and timid little girl. It was a very large church and I didn't know anyone. When my parents took me and Ben to my class with Mrs. Ott (a very kind, grandmotherly woman), I was really nervous. Until then we had attended a teeny-tiny country church with combined grades so that there were a handful of kids in each class. People knew me there, and they knew Ben. But at the new church there was a whole classroom of five-year-olds and no one knew either of us. The kids didn't understand Ben's strange sounds and

---

[1] Jen Boerema "What's this About?" Title Page for "Little Tribe of Benjamin" https://littletribeofbenjamin.wordpress.com/about/

[2] Jen Boerema "Church—Siblings with Special Needs", April 2010 https://littletribeofbenjamin.wordpress.com/2010/04/

unpredictable behavior, and the teacher and helpers didn't know that I could be trusted to make good decisions about handling him. I knew his nonverbal cues, his vocabulary, his patterns, and his trouble spots. For instance, his short attention span would last through a minute of the craft project, and then he'd want to walk around the room and look at a book or "experience" (mess up) someone else's project.

I knew that it was futile to make him sit in a chair for 10 minutes and color a paper plate, and I would suggest that they let him move on to something else, but the teachers would spend all their energy trying to make him do what the rest of the class was doing. After five or ten minutes of quickly escalating threats and demands, he'd get really upset and uncontrollable, and soon my parents would be called. Meanwhile, I was mad because it could have been avoided, and embarrassed because my peers were staring at him. It was not a good way to make friends.

It was also frustrating because I couldn't explain why he was the way he was. After he made babbling sounds, or ripped a page out of a book, ate a crayon, pulled someone's hair, or smeared Elmer's glue on a pink dress, my wide-eyed new friends would ask, "Why does he do that?"

His pediatrician didn't understand it, my parents didn't have any answers, and I certainly couldn't come up with a response that would make sense. I couldn't say, "He has Down syndrome," or "He's Autistic." At least that would've given them a benchmark, something they could relate to. Instead, I became very familiar with the terms "brain damaged" and "mentally impaired," which I chose depending on my audience and my mood.

"Brain damaged" was, in my mind, the best term for kids and teens, although if I felt that they'd get the wrong impression from "damaged," I'd use mentally impaired. I'd start out with "mentally impaired" if I felt like I was dealing with someone who could understand bigger words. Both terms required further explanation and that's where it got tricky.

People were scared of him because he was so strong and unpredictable even as a small boy. I was protective of him and wanted both of us to be accepted, and it was so hard to explain who we were—who he was and who I was with him. He was an intimidating mystery and I was a very quiet girl who wasn't afraid of him. (Well, maybe a little.)

But I didn't have the tools to help them understand my brother and how to interact with him. Even now I still have trouble articulating how Ben is best handled. So much of it depends on the slight variations of his moods; it's so much more art than science. There are general guidelines: use distraction and redirection to change negative behavior, always think two steps ahead to the next activity, anticipate problem situations, be aware of potentially dangerous or undesirable objects nearby, offer plenty of lead-time for changes, and avoid boredom. But it's more than that. It's reading his eyes and recognizing the nanosecond flicker of anxiety or anger. It's knowing whether his eyebrows are furrowed in concentration or frustration. It's listening to his voice and knowing the difference between 'house:' "I don't want to leave" or 'house:' "I'm glad we're all here right now." How do you explain that to someone in a minute?

I don't know. It's probably not possible. So we did the best we could and eventually we both made friends; he more than I. I'm glad for that. There was an army of adults at that church who grew to love Ben, even though we never did work out a good arrangement for Sunday school or Wednesday nights. Those were still hard. But as I got older it did get easier to accept the way he made me different. I got more confident and my skin got thicker.

One bright Sunday morning when I was about 15, our family was walking from the parking lot into church and I was with Ben a little ahead of everyone else. As we neared the big glass double doors, he grabbed my hand and held it as we walked. Then he leaned over and kissed my cheek. I thought for a split second about all the eyes that could be watching us, all my peers who might have seen his ill-timed love, and I almost let go of his hand and wiped my face. But instead I smiled at him and quietly said, "Thank you." We walked a few more steps together holding hands, and I thought about the gift of his love. Then I smiled at the glass doors.

This picture is from the church directory of that new, large church Jen mentions.
Jen was probably seven, Ben five, and Rachel three years of age.

CHAPTER 6

Steadfast

His head hit the brick

"The steadfast love of the Lord never ceases. His mercies never come t an end! They are new every morning. Great is Thy faithfulness, O Lord …" The girls' voices, at five and nine years old, were sweet and confident that morning as we sang those words. It was a happy day as I alternately pushed their swings and pinned articles of clothing and linen to the clothesline.

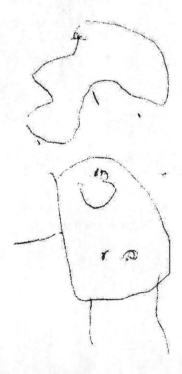

Planting his seven-year-old self butt down and feet out, Ben was deep into "ant investigation," with the subjects of his study climbing over and under his legs. He had a day off from the school he had attended from the age of three. Swishing at any industrious insects hiding in his clothing, I whisked him up, moving him to a grassier spot.

He doesn't and won't understand the words we're singing, I thought. *He understands* love: *our love. But words like* steadfast, faithful, *or* mercy *are way beyond his ability to comprehend.*

Ironically, it was his lack of cognizance and the way it changed *my* life that gave those words such meaning for me. Every day, I clung to God's promises, pleading that his mercy would be new for me and for our family that day.

That night, five-year-old Rachel asked what the word *hypocrites* meant. After I had given her probably too much information, we prayed, and I tucked her into bed. As I tucked Ben in, I realized most of that conversation had also been meaningless to Ben.

When we prayed, did Ben understand anything about who God is? Sure, we taught him to sign "thank you" to Jesus before meals. Did it mean anything? When Ben clasped his hands together before eating, was it a prayer or just a means of getting to his food faster?

While folding another basket of laundry in the silence that evening, I realized that *hypocrite* was a word Ben might never have to understand. I don't think he knows what it is to doubt. His innocence is evident to everyone, and he emulates trust. There is no questioning, no wondering, no faking, no pious actions, just quiet, happy joy—most of the time. In his whole life, Ben will probably never be called a hypocrite. I wish I could say that about myself!

Could he already know what I would never be able to explain? Could he possibly understand God's faithfulness? As we modeled mercy and love, loyalty and steadfastness, I believe he effortlessly trusted in God's attributes—*without questioning*.

Ben has shown me unconditional mercy and love in many of my troubled times. He never remembers an offense. His forgiveness grew my trust in the mercy of God, because Ben's mercy and forgiveness were always new each morning. I've heard that echoed by many parents and siblings of developmentally disabled people.

These memories and the pure faith that Ben exhibited have comforted me through the years. It helps me through times like the incident on Christmas morning 2010. We loved celebrating the day in our big country kitchen, with freshly baked pecan rolls. We usually rearranged furniture so we could enjoy the fireplace on comfy seats and help ourselves to coffee and snacks as we opened presents.

Ben can't relax while others open their gifts, which makes it very hard for the rest of us to enjoy the holiday. So, in more recent years we shifted to opening our presents without Ben. In the group home where Ben lives, their tradition is for all the guys to open their presents on Christmas morning too, so it has worked out well. After we enjoyed the morning, his siblings would hop in the van for the new tradition of picking up Ben together. Then, the minute he walks in the door, Ben can open his presents without interruption.

And from the pictures, it looks like he was enjoying himself on that Christmas morning, A brightly colored, light-up Buzz Lightyear bedcover is lying across his lap, and he is sporting new sunglasses. I see Walt Disney's *A Bug's Life* DVD and a new winter hat in one of the pictures.

I didn't realize that the chandelier would be a problem. We had moved the table away from it, and Ben was not used to being able to walk under it. Or maybe his new blanket was lying on the floor and tripping him up. But when Ben stood up, he couldn't catch his balance and fell backward—all 250 pounds of him—onto the brick hearth.

The next moments were horrendous. Ben's eyes were rolled back into his head, and he was unresponsive. Ed said later that he thought Ben was dead. I think all of us wondered. If the fall hadn't killed him, I was terrified he'd bleed to death from the amount of blood gushing from his head.

Thankfully, Rachel had first aid and CPR training, and was more accustomed to trauma than any of us. She gave directions and cared for Ben. We ran for towels and cleared a path for the paramedics, who responded within minutes.

Ben did regain consciousness. He was very scared of it all, whimpering as they bound up the wound and wrapped gauze around the top of his head and ending around his chin. The paramedics left quite soon, knowing we would be heading out for the hospital ASAP.

To this day, I don't know why I insisted on going with Ben. Rachel was the only medically trained person among us, yet I told her to stay home. I was probably trying to salvage Christmas Day for them. Had I been thinking straight, I would have insisted Rachel ride with Ed to the hospital, in case there were complications on the way. Hysteria does crazy things. I obviously proved again that I have a hard time relinquishing my role as mother to Ben. I didn't give Rachel—an adult by then—the respect she deserved either.

By the time we were finished at the hospital, Ben had become playful, tickling the hands of nurses who checked his vitals or pulling the sheet over his eyes to initiate peekaboo. The staff got to know the comedian he is. I took the liberty, then, to very sincerely ask, "Doctor, will Ben be able to speak when the injury is healed?" He stopped for a moment, unsure how to answer, then laughed along with us as we enjoyed a Christmas joke.

That was one of the first times Ben fell. Over the next few years, there were more incidents. One study's results appeared to say that his blood pressure dropped when he stood up too fast. He would go down backwards, usually, hitting his head on the edge of the kitchen counter, table, or whatever was in the way.

A specialist later determined that Ben should try ankle and foot orthoses (AFOs). (It's a brace that covers the bottom of Ben's foot, with hinges at the ankles attached to a large piece of plastic-like material that rides up the back of his leg and gets buckled around the front of his shin.) He has worn AFOs every day for some years now, and they have made a considerable difference in his stability. There has been a marked decrease in falls, but sadly, not an end to them.

If I ever wondered about the necessity for the braces, I found out afresh recently, when Ed and I took Ben bowling. I took his braces off and put his bowling shoes on. I put his smiley-faced bowling ball in his arms when he stood up.

As Ben walked along the approach, his bowling ball started slipping from his arms. And as that weight shifted, he started falling backward. Thankfully, I was able to right him before the fall, but bowling was ended for that day. He was too scared of falling again.

We did find out there's a place in town that lets their customers wear their own shoes. Done!

CHAPTER 7

Therapeutic Volunteers

They raced alongside the mat

A very active Ben was seven years old when we began therapy with volunteers, at home. Ben continually pulled himself along with his forearms, doing the army crawl until he was two years of age. I had asked if home therapy might be helpful, but Ben's first pediatrician—as was his attitude most of the time—didn't give it any credence. At seven, Ben still fell and struggled with his balance, toddling precariously.

But I never forgot Barbie! Years earlier, my aunt had invited relatives and church friends to help with a patterning therapy program for her daughter, Barbie, who is more severely disabled than Ben. My mother and one of my sisters were faithful volunteers. We all knew that with the severity of her challenges, Barbie would probably never have walked without the hard, dedicated work of her parents and all the volunteers who had helped on a daily basis more than fifteen years prior.

While Ben had fantastic therapists at Ottawa Area Center, his speech was limited to babble. Doctors had no suggestions, and regular schools had no protocol or special therapies. We felt we needed to try this hope toward a more normal life. Our exhausting family routine, though, made the kind of commitment needed seem impossible. After much prayer, an old hymn, "Day by Day," gave me my answer one Sunday morning. When I looked it up later, the promise in its lyrics came from Deuteronomy 33:25 (NIV): "As your days, so shall your strength be." That is precisely how it worked out!

We needed a minimum of three people per session. All we had to do was ask. Friends and acquaintances heard about it and volunteered, once or twice each week, to help Ben.

We often traveled to Ohio with Ben and our other children then, watching, learning, and being trained at a clinic near Dayton. The mission statement on the website of what is now the

Rehabilitation Center of the Hahn-Hufford Center of Hope[3] reads in part, "Serving infants, children, and adults who are experiencing difficulties associated with stroke, birth trauma, Traumatic Brain Injury, Cerebral Palsy, Autism, Down Syndrome and others; our mission is to help each client reach their maximum potential."

That's what we wanted to do, help Ben reach his maximum potential. Of course, we had no idea then of the extent of Ben's disabilities and had an unrealistic idea of where the maximum would eventually fall. At that time Ben's diagnosis may still have been EMI (Educable Mental Impairment), not TMI (Trainable), or certainly not the SMI (Severe) category that became more accurate over the years.

Hardworking professionals at the clinic warned us we would need scores of volunteers to make home therapy work. Four people were needed for the table. On each side, a team member would alternately bring Ben's hand forward, slide it back as they lifted his knee, slide it forward and push the knee back, and repeat. Another team member held his feet tightly, keeping them in the right position for creeping. A fourth person gently cushioned his head between their hands, training it, smoothly but firmly, to the other side when that arm came forward.

We were retraining his brain to crawl the correct way. Among other things, therapy also trained him in motor skills he had missed in his development. We were, of course, hopeful it would improve his intelligence and his lack of speech.

A large wooden rectangle consumed our tiny kitchen. We called it "the patterning table." We lived in a basement-less, two-bedroom home—our first—housing our family of five. The table boasted massive two-by-sixes, forty-five inches in width and six feet in length, standing about four feet high. Covering its top were nearly four inches of firm foam rubber under a layer of vinyl upholstery, which rounded the corners and edges and kept it easy to wash. Ben's grandpa, my dad, built the patterning table to specific dimensions so we could stand alongside without bending over too much. We also rolled out a fifteen-foot-long, thirty-six-inch-wide runner, made from that same vinyl, which coursed through the living room and down the bedroom hall.

Many of our friends sang happy songs to Ben during therapy, and some quoted Scripture, hoping to calm him. Working just as hard to distract him were the children of our friends, theatrically "dying" in response to shots from his pretend gun, and making silly faces, and challenging his speed as they raced alongside the mat.

I now know what a significant time that was for Ed and me. We experienced incredible love and support from friends and family. We knew it would all be worth it.

I treasure a photo of my dad with his sleeves rolled up and his thick, factory-toughened working hands—the same hands that played sweet music on a musical saw—encouraging his grandson. First, Dad labored over the construction of that massive table. He built it to last forever. (We had to

---

[3] HAHN-HUFFORD CENTER OF HOPE Rehabilitation Center for Neurological Development, http://www.rcnd.org

saw it apart to dismantle it eventually!) Then Dad worked with Ben's wildly kicking feet when others couldn't be there, though he never thought he was "good at it." In the photo, he is encouraging Ben to apply the creeping lessons on the mat, threatening him with a scary-grandpa growl if Ben slowed down too soon.

Four years later, Dad refinished an extra-long oak bed frame for Ben's eleventh birthday in March, though Dad was suffering severe lower back pain. We found out he was battling pancreatic cancer. He passed away in December, a few short weeks after greeting Ben's new little brother, James Matthew.

This story brings back many memories of my mom, too. She not only helped with therapy at our house but worked with Ben on her living room floor whenever she babysat. She coaxed him to crawl and creep the correct way long before we began therapy. She had a hard time coming to terms with the facts of Ben's disabilities. "Working at it" was the way she dealt with life, and work she did! She wanted us to try patterning therapy long before I could admit the need for it. She understood its value. We all missed her visits to our homes as she aged—she was either canning with/for us, or ironing, or sewing! She's been in heaven a decade now, but I can still feel her love and support, as well as Dad's. I know Ben misses them.

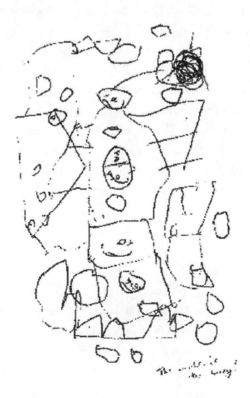

This drawing is what patterning might have looked like to Ben: loads of smiling faces, arms that wouldn't give him a break, and contraptions to lie and creep on. An essential element of therapy was desensitizing Ben to touch so that others could help him learn and grow without triggering constant, compulsive overreactions. He giggled a lot and cried when we used soft brushes and other pliable gadgets to sweep up and down his limbs. Cornstarch powder and repetition helped us calm his impulsive body.

I don't remember all the arguments for stimulating the vestibular part of his inner ear, but I do remember Ed drilling bolts into the door frame between the bedroom wing and the living room of that little old house. They had to be big enough to hold large metal clamps on either side of the frame. First, we fastened Ben's feet into the contraption; then we helped him swing and circle upside down. There were many facets of the therapy program that we did not use, but we did hang Ben upside down for gradually increasing minutes. He learned to love it.

I watched many people give their best for Ben's hoped-for progress. He had learned to walk long before we started therapy, but often fell. We believe therapy helped his balance. Certainly the falls became less frequent.

In the special education school Ben attended, and more recently in his adult foster care (AFC) home, some of the same desensitizing techniques were used at the advice of his occupational therapist, with calming effects. Wearing a weighted vest was very helpful for a time also.

I know those early therapy years for Ben were a considerable factor in the career choices made by his younger sisters. Rachel, as I mentioned earlier, is an occupational therapist. She identifies the brightly colored balls and swings, vibrant steps, and mirrors in the therapy room at Ottawa Area Center as pivotal to her calling. She and her older sister, Jen, were two of Ben's biggest boosters in our home, often encouraging him to do things on his own.

His younger sister, Aubrey, master's degree as a Certified Therapeutic Recreation Specialist. She is also a Certified PATH International Registered Instructor, and founded a therapeutic horseback riding non-profit for people with physical, cognitive, and emotional disabilities and struggles. Ben's youngest sibling, James, has committed at least six years of his life to serving our country in the army, hoping to protect the freedoms we all cherish, including the ones that protect lives like Ben's. These are some of the gifts our family received from Ben, preparing them for lives of service.

Though it's over twenty-five years later, I still remember those volunteers with gratitude. One supportive couple was in their seventies, yet faithfully came to help. A few of my girlfriends came with their young children. The children stared with big eyes of fear at first, then learned to encourage and play. I know Ben's big smile and squawky complaints have a special place in their memory banks!

CHAPTER 8

To Trust or Not

I used to be stronger!

Many people have experienced unanswered prayer—or prayer answered in a way that wasn't the hope. We prayed too, often with fasting, and definitely with fervor. We prayed in faith, believing that healing Ben was not too hard for God. But it felt like the puzzle of faith just didn't come together, like the random pieces in this drawing. We had lots of wonderful times in prayer, spent with passionate, wise friends using heartfelt, words, right from the Bible. But Ben still did not talk, and he was falling further and further behind.

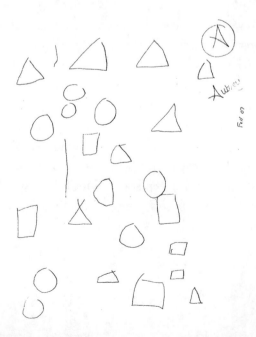

Aubrey was born ten years after Ben, and a little brother followed her. When she sat with Ben as he drew this picture in the fall of 2007, she was fourteen and he was twenty-four. She gave Ben some direction as he drew this picture (you'll notice her signature, and the circled "A"). The triangles are probably his attempt to mimic her initial. The objects—squares, triangles, and circles—are otherwise random and disconnected—a little like Ben's brain and the way he processes things.

We love the story in Mark 7:32-36 (NIV) where Jesus healed the young man who could not speak. When we tucked Ben into bed at night we prayed "that his tongue [would be] loosed and he [begin] to speak plainly."

Sometimes we read the King James Version of this passage as well: "And he took him aside from the multitude, and put his fingers into his ears, and he spit and touched his tongue." (In case you're wondering, we never followed *that* formula.) Then… listen… when Jesus "looked up to heaven, he sighed." I *love* that! I love the whole story. First, Jesus "took him aside from the multitude," showing the man respect, and giving him privacy and undivided attention. Then Jesus sighed.

Did Jesus groan? I wondered. Or did he sigh and take in a massive breath of God, of faith, and of grace before speaking healing? I've come to think of his sigh as more like mine, when I feel burdened for Ben. "He sighed, and saith unto him, 'Ephphatha,' that is, *be opened*. And straightway his ears were opened, and the *string of his tongue was loosed*."

How often and how passionately we prayed that the string of Ben's tongue would be loosed! I would quote chapter 7:37 (KJV) then: they "were beyond measure astonished, saying, *He hath done all things well (emphasis mine)*: He maketh both the deaf to hear …" I would pause there. Ben would grin, and I would repeat, "He maketh both the deaf to hear and—"

"*Beh!*" Ben would bellow.

I'd smile, "Yes, he makes Ben to speak."

But later, stifling groans in the dark, I wrestled. *God! I want to be the one who exclaims, "He hath done all things well." I would, God, I would tell everyone! Please God, why not Ben?*

The testimonies and stories of parents with disabled children who trust God right from the beginning never cease to amaze me. They seem to have no doubts! No questions! No struggling!

It wasn't that way with us. We thought we had birthed a healthy son. Nothing in my pregnancy or his birth said otherwise. The two-year discovery of something very different left us with many unanswered questions.

With each year something did grow incrementally, but it wasn't faith. *Resentment* grew into my companion. Ben at six years old still didn't have a natural clock in his brain. That wouldn't develop until around his tenth birthday. He was awake most of the night. We managed to live on three- to five-hour segments of uninterrupted sleep.

Normal achievements like sleeping through the night, practicing independent bathroom skills, relaxing instead of going ballistic with a babysitter, learning the alphabet, riding a bike, going to school, reading, writing, buttoning buttons, talking, and understanding safety rules on a street were not happening with Ben. Instead, the gap between Ben and his peers became a gaping chasm.

Any slight progress reports were praises we sent to our prayer partners. But inwardly we wondered what was wrong with our faith and when we should give up. "He hath done all things well." *Really*? Could I agree with that? *Hypocrite!* I convicted myself. Rather than risk crediting God with a faulty design, I blamed Satan for Ben's IQ. *No,* I silently argued, *Ben was not done well, God!*

The promises of faith healing made it sound to us like Ben's healing was up to us, that it depended on *our* faith. Wealth was promised as well, yet we continued to live in a two-bedroom, cement-block home with three children. We were praying and we were believing—we thought—but we seemed to be begging to an *impotent* god.

I had suffered one miscarriage by this point and had undergone back surgery. The surgery was due in part to a car accident, but aggravated by the extra lifting and other challenges associated with Ben's life.

Ed's body also began to reflect a level of physical and spiritual exhaustion. Ed worked long weeks—a minimum of 47.5 hours—for an automotive supplier for Detroit's Big Three automobile manufacturers in the high-pressure 1980s automotive design world. Whenever he finally caught some sleep, he would wake up repeatedly, gasping for breath and feeling like he was being strangled. (it sounded exactly like that too.)

It was a dark and stormy night of the soul for us when Ed came to the end of hope. Sorrow, sleep deprivation, and the constant demands of his job had weakened him. In total despair, his voice rasping, he cried out to the cold walls of our drafty little house, "What do we have to do? Do we have to cut ourselves like Baal worshippers to get God to listen? God's blessing is supposed to be ours, not this endless curse!" I knew he was referring to the history of Elijah on Mount Carmel as written in I Kings 18:21(NIV) "Elijah went before the people and said, "How long will you waver between two opinions? If the Lord is God, follow him; but if Baal is God, follow him." The prophets of Baal couldn't get their god to listen to them so they began cutting themselves—which didn't get a response either!

As in the days of Elijah, only God could answer Ed. But God was wretchedly silent that night. I had lost another child and was confined to bed rest. I didn't even try to answer Ed's frightening questions. They were too deep, too personal, and way too terrifying.

After several deathlike hours, Ed walked resolutely back into the living room. I remember only that he had his Bible in his hand, and that he chose his words very carefully. Purposefully sitting down in a rocking chair, he faced me, looking into my eyes. His own were red-rimmed. In a quavering voice, he said, "'Though he slay me, yet will I trust him…'" Job 13:15a (KJV)

I knew, though borrowed from Job, this was Ed's very own faith statement. With absolute certainty, he told me that even if he lost his life in this battle, he would *not* deny God. "I will worship him and him alone, regardless if God *ever* chooses to heal Ben or not."

I didn't tell Ed right then, but God had spoken to my heart that same afternoon. The message was sweet and tender, and came through music, as it often does. For the next year, it seemed I heard "My Redeemer Is Faithful and True" (by Steven Curtis Chapman) several times each day. Just hopping in the car to run an errand, I'd turn on the radio, and S.C.Chapman would jump in with me!

There have been many terrifyingly hard times since that day, and I am grateful Ed has never wavered on that commitment. Many times, he's been a rock when my faith falters. I remember how precariously close we came to losing God's gift of faith during those hard years. We have a real bond with people who question God's promises.

I think we may have been demanding something apart from God's will, rather than choosing to *trust* him. There is nothing simple about trusting. It is often where Satan causes the breach. In fact, it's a pretty tired old tool: *Did God really say* [fill in the blank]*?* Then doubts and despair move in, and bitterness grows.

During one whole year I prayed, "May the God of hope fill you with all joy and peace as you trust in him, so that you may overflow with hope by the power of the Holy Spirit" Rom. 15:13 (NIV). Daily—sometimes hourly—I prayed, "God, you said you are the God of hope. *Please* fill me with joy and peace as I try to trust in you, Lord! So that I can overflow with *hope*. I don't feel any hope, Lord! It will have to be by the power of the Holy Spirit." That prayer readily comes to my lips to this day. Since that time, I have given that verse to many people or written it in cards when I felt they might be fighting for hope.

Years later, when our younger son was four, Ed held James's head an arm's length away while James tried to "beat him up." James was getting frustrated and complained, "I used to be stronger!" Ed replied, "Until you met up with me!"

That image of Ed or me fighting God, while totally oblivious to who we were fighting, and how out sized we were, comes back to make us smile. Trusting while not understanding eventually helped us believe that God could even choose to make Ben, with all Ben's limitations, for God's purposes. God's statement to Moses helped us also: "Who gave human beings their mouths? Who makes them deaf or mute? Who gives them sight or makes them blind? Is it not I the Lord?" Exodus 4:11 (NIV)

The decision to trust God opened the doors to envisioning and believing God's call on Ben's life. God even gave me a vision once of the multitude of people Ben has known, and influenced—more than I would never know. We caught a glimpse of Ben's unique place in God's plan, not just ours.

As we consciously placed our hope in God, God increased and strengthened our weakened faith. We have to give up and even fight those fears about Ben's care, and all of the questions about the future. We choose to let God answer—or not—as he sees fit.

That despair, and the total lack of sleep (or sanity), can undoubtedly lead to depression. Medication became necessary at times when I could not lift the weight. I don't know your situation.

I know mine felt totally unmanageable. Check with your doctor and be honest with them about your life circumstances and how you're feeling. There are natural supplements, too, and I'm using that currently.

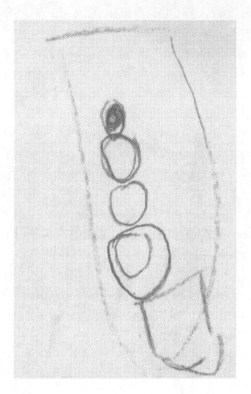

This sketch reminds me of a stoplight. When we're driving, I often ask Ben what I need to do when the light turns red. He quickly throws his hand forward and out, signing *Stop*! Interestingly, in this drawing he colored each circle with a red line and filled in the top one with a red color. It reminds me: *Stop questioning*! *Stop fretting*! *Stop the fear*! *Trust*!

CHAPTER 9

Visions of Sugar Plums

Our very own Christmas guests

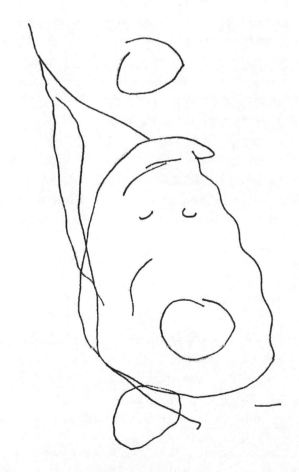

Christmas is always full of magic for me. I still feel like a child when lights twinkle and the aroma of special treats or candles fills the house. When our first three children were very young, I wanted to give them a memory that would help them feel that way too.

After the children finally fell asleep, one wintry December night so long ago, I asked Ed to humor me. (He was used to my irrational behavior by then.) Together we woke and bundled our sleepy, shocked children to face the winter's chill.

Gusts of smoke from the woodstove and swirls of snow greeted us as we stepped through the front door amid giggles and gasps of joy. We trudged all the way to the road, then counted "One … two …. three!" We turned around to ooh and aah over the magical lights strung around the outside and inside of our tiny cedar-sided home. Huddled together, our breath circled us as we took in the sensations of this night.

Conspiratorially, I asked them all (including Ed) to memorize the sight of twinkling stars overhead, snowflakes falling, the white, frosty moon, glittering lights, and the inviting whiff of smoke puffing out of the chimney. Five-year-old Rachel—twirling and frolicking—was almost lost to a snowbank. Jenny couldn't stop grinning, her sparkling eyes dancing with excitement, taking in every bit of that sensory experiment. I asked them to close their eyes then and remember everything they were experiencing. One at a time—when I was sure they weren't peeking—I popped a tiny piece of candy cane on each tongue, shouting, "Surprise!" Then we huddled closer and sang "Silent Night."

After kicking our way back through the snow, we opened that same front door to become our very own Christmas guests. Daddy opened up James Herriot's *The Christmas Day Kitten* by the crackling woodstove. By seeing, hearing, tasting, feeling, and even smelling the winter air, I hoped they would always remember the magic of Christmas.

Ed and I tucked the children back into bed. We held the Advent Book open so everyone could see it, opening the first window for nine-year-old Jenny to read. In those early years, we were pretty religious about opening only one little window each night, slowly unveiling the old story. It still acts as a small part of the Christmas traditions in our home, though its dramatized story is treated with a great deal of sacrilegious humor!

I leaned in for a kiss as I tucked Ben in that night. He pointed to his mouth with a glint in his eyes. "Did you like the candy, Ben?" I asked.

"Yah!" He giggled and squeezed me tightly.

"You're welcome, little elf!"

Now, many years later, when I see my adult children's eyes turn into the sparkling, eager eyes of children, I'm reminded of the magic of that Christmas night. As I edit this story in December 2017, many years after the events took place, the magic has grown. I now get to enjoy the sparkle in our grandchildren's eyes when I bake Christmas cookies—which happens every time they visit—throughout the month! In truth, Jen and their daddy, Kelvin, do a fabulous job of putting the sparkle in their eyes without Grandma's help.

Our vivacious Rachel, who lives and works in California, pursues that magic by driving up to the mountain home of her special friends, where she has the loving distinction of being the "adopted daughter" and "older sister." I can see her eyes dance with her *other* family.

Our youngest, James, is stationed in Fairbanks, Alaska. I pray the magic of Christmas will somehow seep into the cracks in his noisy cement barracks so far from home.

For Ben, the minute Halloween is over, he starts signing "tree" with fingertips together, pointing up, excitedly whispering one syllable: "ice." It happens *every* time we see him—*every* morning when he wakes and *many* times each day—until Christmas! When we take him to his home after visits between October 31 and December 25, the patient staff in his home tell us the same story, I wonder: *Could I have overdone it?*

CHAPTER 10

Muhmuh, Dah, and a Ten-Year-Old

Shooting two guns at imaginary enemies

There's no way to prepare a marriage for the entrance of a child with special needs. Ben grew very tall. But he remained an infant and toddler in speech and development. As I've mentioned, he didn't even sleep through the night until he was around ten years old.

According to a November 29, 2017, article on disabilityscoop.com[4], the CDC says that developmental disabilities are on the rise. "Between 2014 and 2016, the prevalence of developmental disabilities among kids ages 3 to 17 increased from 5.76 percent to 6.99 percent, according to figures … from the U.S. Centers for Disease Control and Prevention." If that is true, more parents are going to experience special needs in their children.

I didn't put much stock into the Intelligence Quotient (IQ) tests when Ben was little, and I don't know if I ever found out what IQ my other children have, but I found it helpful when I was trying to figure out where Ben fit with other children and when his diagnosis changed from "trainably" mentally impaired (today that would be a "mild" diagnosis) to "Moderately" impaired and last, as he got older, to "Severe." I needed to know what it meant, and how they came to that conclusion. Being objective, as a parent, is hardly possible. This is one of the facts and figures that helped me understand Ben's limitations, how we could get the help and services he needed—for life—and helped me accept where those limitations were going to be, and why.

When your child's disability is given a name, you have a better idea of what to expect or plan

---

[4] Shaun Heasley, "CDC says "Developmental Disabilities Are On the Rise" *disabilityscoop.com* November 29, 2017, https://www.disabilityscoop.com/2017/11/29/cdc-disabilities-rise/24468/)

for. With Ben, they didn't have a diagnosis, only the guess that a virus attacked his brain and left him with global developmental delays. We had no others to compare him to, so the IQ test helped us understand. Each child is different, so I'll just explain the use of it, as I understand it, and this study, written by Samantha Gluck, August, 2016[5] is a really good place to start!

She reports, experts divide the types of cognitive impairment into four categories: mild intellectual disability, moderate intellectual disability, severe intellectual disability, and profound intellectual disability. The degree of impairment from an <u>intellectual disability</u> varies widely. DSM-V places less emphasis on the degree of impairment (i.e. IQ scores) and more on the amount and type of intervention needed.

While IQ scores are still relevant and important in assessing the level of intellectual disability, the new DSM-V adds another layer of diagnostic criteria (*Intellectual Disability: Causes and Characteristics*). Mental health professionals must consider the person's ability or impairment across three skill areas: conceptual, social, and practical life skill."

Reading the whole article is helpful, but I've abbreviated it to listing those four categories, based on IQ tests:

1. Mild Impairment with an IQ of 50-70
2. Moderate Impairment   35-49
3. Severe Impairment (Ben's category of 20-34) and those with an IQ of
4. less than 20: Profound Intellectual Disabilities.

Please know that many of the things I share about Ben's disabilities may never be the reality for most parents of special needs children, In this study they have found that only three to four percent of all persons with Intellectual Disabilities are at the "Severe" designation, where Ben is diagnosed. There are, however, many with worse physical disabilities than Ben!

Our hearts go out to these young parents, especially the ones in states or countries where there is little help from the community. It is our hope and prayer they will find encouragement in these pages to stay the course, find a community of faith that will help them, and also find a way to protect or fight for their marriage.

For those parenting a special needs child and other children on your own—and I know too many of you who do—I offer my admiration and continue to pray God sends all that you need and friends to help. I hope we'll be able to connect, via the website. For those who know families like this, please jump In to help!

---

[5] Samantha Gluck, "Mild, Moderate, Severe Intellectual Disability Differences", https://www.healthyplace.com/neurodevelopmental-disorders/intellectual-disability/mild-moderate-severe-intellectual-disability-differences

I'm pretty sure Ed is the one with the tie here. And, of course, I'm the one with the halo! Ben drew these characters one Sunday when we sat in church together.

I remember one specialist visually placing his hands close together, then describing how that space would become an ever-widening gap between Ben and his peers. He stretched his hands as far apart as they could go.

That is precisely what happened. Ben just quit mentally maturing. He spent years in toddlerhood, especially in skills like potty training. When I study the not-so-lovely tantrums of our two-year-old grandchild, I realized many of Ben's responses stayed at that developmental level right into adulthood.

I found a great quotation, and I'd like to give credit to the owner, but my searches only show it listed as "anonymous" or "unknown":

> "Marriage is like jogging through a puddle of industrial strength rubber glue. You can work hard and make it through the struggles, but you usually leave your bobby socks and sneakers behind along the way."

Having owned and painted an eighteen by thirty-six feet cement pool several times with rubber paint, we know a little about trashed sneakers! Ed and I both feel like we've jogged through quite a few of those glutinous puddles in our forty-plus years of marriage. You could say those marriage vows were *stretched* many times by the demands of caring for Ben, and the exhaustion that came with it. A relaxed life was impossible. (We were parenting other children too, and I had several miscarriages during the early years.)

I have always cherished a quotation from our pastor's prayer as we knelt at an old prayer bench, following our vows. Since then I've learned it was written by Matthew Henry: "Women were created from the rib of man to be beside him, not from his head to top him, nor from his feet to be trampled by him, but from under his arm to be protected by him, near to his heart to be loved by him."[6] It is a word picture of how I've felt about my relationship with Ed through these challenging years.

It took many years for me to understand the enormity of Ed's emotions. Ben was our firstborn son—I know now what a painful loss that is for a man. Working ten-hour days or more in a very demanding job and dealing with the mania that Ben created made for a pressure-cooker existence. Neither one of us could honestly know what the other was experiencing, and even if we had, there often just wasn't any extra energy to give to the other.

We sat together in a Sunday school class one morning without Ben (which was memorable by itself). The teacher wanted us to list ten things we didn't like about our spouses. I'm ashamed to say I got right to work, listing a few things that did bug me. Glancing over at Ed, I caught his tender look and watched him tuck his pen in his shirt pocket. He'd invented some ridiculous things, like "she doesn't chop the wood small enough" and "when she changes the oil in the car, she spills it."

"You and I are in a war," he said later. "We need each other to survive. I will *never* attack you, especially over little things." In the three decades since then, he has worked to maintain that loyalty—and believe me, I've tested it!

There are many obstacles, little or significant, to intimacy and growth in any marriage, regardless if there are disabilities or not. Often, all Ed and I needed was to be close or to spend an hour or two alone while our parents helped with the children. Sometimes the best we could do was to take the hand we knew so well, haul each other out of the latest sticky mess, and leave the sneakers behind!

Even now, our habit—at the least—is to hold one another's hand as soon as we get into bed each night—often to pray, but most often for the comfort and assurance it gives us of the love—and the struggles and worries we share. By God's grace, we hope to continue that tradition for many more years.

The journal entries I wrote from those years, like the following, have helped us recall shared memories that deepen our love. Writing is the way I processed many milestones of those years, and I believe it was helpful to Ed that I didn't "process" all those thoughts with him!

---

6 Deen Carnes, Matthew Henry quote, *Reformed Spirit Blogspot.com,* December 9, 2016, https://reformedspirit. blogspot.com/2016/12/women-were-created-from-rib-of-man-to.html

On the Eve of Ben's Tenth Birthday
A Journal Entry

The eve of your tenth birthday—I write to remember. I write to believe it. I write to know and understand.

How I'd love to write a book that makes you a hero to other boys—a person they would aspire to be. *Who would a hero be like for you?* I wonder. *If I could ask you, what would you say?* Who is idolized by most ten-year-old boys? A baseball star? A rock star? A football legend?

I think your hero would be your dad. I see it when you scream and run out the closest door as your dad's "little yellow beep-beep" comes into the yard. "Dah-Dah!" you screech, high, like a blue jay's persistent call. How would a "normal" ten-year-old greet his father at the end of a day? A grunt, a view of the back of a head turned to a video game? A "Hi, Dad, you won't believe what happened at school …" Probably some sons ignore that arrival altogether. Few bestow such a cloak of love and distinction as our Ben, without saying one word other than, "Dah!"

Tonight, when Daddy came home, it was dark out already. But you were there, running to greet him before he had the car door open. You're always there, as he has been for you. It was so mild for March 30 in Michigan, where sixty degrees is like a summer night. The out-of-doors has been quiet for so long. Tonight it was awakened. The spring peeper called to her friends, the tree frogs, all around our woodsy property. What a cacophony of music! We listened for a while, and now, as I sit in the rocker with your little sister, I hear them in the night. They woke up just in time to wish you a happy birthday, Ben!

The woodland creatures watched you, the big boy who rambles in all kinds of weather, playing with his sisters or enjoying his solitude. What do you think as you play for hours, summer or winter, seeming never to get tired or chilled? Wandering along, you pick up sticks, play in the water of early spring, make makeshift boats, or sled over the frozen winter pond.

Swinging on the bag swing in all weather, you turn the leaf-covered sand into mud in the spring, and smooth, dirty ice in the winter. When cars pass, you wave. If anyone walks or rides by, you stand and stare, unabashed, startling them with your "Hahee!" The mature white pines weep to hear the words from the lips of boys or girls who have yet to learn compassion.

You love your scooter, especially in the spring, when it's waited in the basement all winter for you to ride. Could this be the year you learn to ride a two-wheeler? Since you outgrew your favorite Hot Wheel several years ago, your only bike has been the backseat of the tandem. You've gotten very good at that, even shooting two guns at imaginary enemies! I love driving and catching the surprised faces of pedestrians greeted by my son. You only feel the need to grab the handlebar when the driver begins to tip.

Other years I thought so much about your *lack* of progress and *lack* of mental growth. I would look up and down the toy aisles, hoping for something that you would enjoy. Something that didn't say, "For ages zero to three." This year it wasn't quite as hard.

Tonight, I say a birthday prayer instead, just thanking him for you. Happy birthday, beautiful boy! I pray God will gift you with kind friends and one surprise package of acceptance. I know the creatures great and small echo their love and wish for your joy.

Happy birthday, dear boy of ten!

CHAPTER 11

Sister Number One

A purple bunny and … a gray mouse

So much of Ben's joy comes from moments shared with his sisters. When he was young, many important memories for the girls involved Ben's peers and teachers. They looked forward to Ben's school's festivals and family days. It gave them a unique perspective on the world while sharing fun events with their brother too.

Ben's two oldest sisters were homeschooled. In part, I chose this because Ben demanded so much attention. I wanted the girls to have my time when Ben was at school. We also wanted them to become more educated and compassionate than we had been, by gaining unique exposure to Ben's world.

Jen was two and a half years old, and Ben was nine months old for this Christmas pose. Jen supported him so he could sit up, because he couldn't sit up on his own. Jen is still one of his excellent support persons (and stand-in legal guardian).

Ben's relationships with those two sisters—one older than he, the other younger—remained very close through the years. Whenever Ben came home from his adult foster care home in 2004–2005, the first telephone call would be to his older sister Jen, living in Croatia at that time. I'd try to surprise her and get his big booming voice on before she knew who was calling.

"Hahee!" he would yell, many decibels louder than a normal voice, eyes sparkling, gripping the phone tightly to his ear. He listened intently to her voice, with a hint of a tear waiting to brim. He had no idea she was on a different continent. He just knew he missed her. She wasn't at our house, which he signed by putting his fingertips together in the shape of a roof and pointing to the spot next to him, where he wanted her to be.

Before she left, Jen had said she was most worried about staying connected with Ben because of his lack of words. Their form of communication is a big hug and lots of smiles. She understands each movement he makes and needs no interpretation—when she is with him. She missed him very much, but phone conversations didn't last long.

"How are you, Ben?"

"Guh!"

Then I would interject something he'd done in school or his foster care home, and Jen would act like she'd been there and was excited about what he'd done.

After about twenty seconds of silence, she would say, "Bye, Ben, I love you."

"Ah yah yah!" (I love you) he would reply through giggles, then wait for another goodbye, then add "Buh!"

Nowadays when we phone Jen, Ben also gets a greeting from his brother-in-law Kelvin, or his little niece and nephew. His excitement triples as their enthusiasm for the screen mirrors his own!

We're not surprised that his sister Rachel is involved with patient advocacy and placement. She was a fierce advocate for Ben and took Ben's goals seriously, working relentlessly to help him make progress. Jen and Rachel each played the part of Ben's escort to his annual school prom, pampering him all evening. His friends were jealous of his beautiful girlfriends.

Often now, it's the sister who's ten years younger, Aubrey, who drives out to pick up Ben on Sundays when he visits, labeling their selfies "Sunday Funday."

I pegged this as Ben's self-portrait with an angel—his sisters are that to him, in many ways.

Below, I include an excerpt of a letter Jen wrote to Ben when she was nineteen years old. It speaks for itself about their relationship. Ben would have been about 17 at the time of this writing. It begins with a prologue:

> This letter was written to my younger brother Ben, who has been mentally impaired since birth. He is seventeen and looks like all other normal teenage boys, but he acts more like a three-year-old. He can't talk, read, or write, but he's taught me much about patience, gentleness, hope, and faith. I think that publishing this letter will give other college students a better understanding of handicapped people and their families.
>
> April 2000
>
> Dear Ben,
>
> So many things came to mind when I thought about writing a letter to you. It's not easy to put my thoughts on paper. Where do I start? And what do I want to tell you?
>
> Maybe I should just say that I love you—I love you even though some people would say that you're more work than you're worth and that I'll never see any results from loving you.

Maybe I should tell you all the reasons *why* I love you. Sometimes I lose sight of them, but when I can see clearly again, there they are, the same as always.

First, your smile. Big, silly, and accompanied by a hearty laugh; or soft and trusting; or (the one I like best) the mischievous one that brings out the sparkle in your eyes. And you never let me forget that, do you? You may not be "normal," but you still know how to push my buttons! We've shared so many things together: Roller skating at the rink with your class, hanging on to the wall together so we wouldn't fall. Dressing up for Halloween in our costumes Mom made for us, me as a purple bunny and you as a grey mouse. Going to Sunday School together (oh, how I hated it when the teachers thought they knew how to handle you better than I did!). Playing our version of cops and robbers. Taking bike rides together (remember the tandem?). …

Fourth, your extreme silliness when we are together. You love to play hide-and-go-seek, but your idea of hiding is to stand behind me with your hands on my shoulders, crouch down a little, and ask (in your language, of course) "Where's Ben?". It's getting hard to hide your six-foot-200-pound body behind me! At other times your face-contorting expressions make me laugh out loud with you. I can almost imagine you're normal when you act like that.

Fifth, your gentleness with people who are hurting. Sometimes when I have had a bad day, and I'm trying not to cry when I say goodnight to you, you instinctively reach to hug me. You look at me a little bit confused, and sad, and try to make me smile by hiding under the covers.

Those are a few of the reasons I love you. But that's not all I really wanted to say. Maybe I should tell you *how* I love you. There's all the normal ways—hugs and kisses, saying the words, writing notes for you when you go away so your respite giver can read them to you—but I also get to love you in a way that most people don't. I share the hurts you don't deserve. I have seen all the stares, and pointing fingers heard the whispered comments, and felt the isolation of being "different."

I saw the way people looked at us one Sunday morning when you reached for my hand as we walked into the church. Teenage siblings aren't supposed to act that way, but you didn't know that. You still like to give me kisses on the cheek sometimes at inappropriate times, and people still look, but I don't mind anymore. You're just proud to have me as a sister.

I heard the sarcastic remarks made at family gatherings about the trips to a special doctor for you: "Guess he needs to go to that doctor some more. It sure hasn't helped yet." We were willing to try anything that might help you be more normal. And their ignorance of who you are and what you have to offer them! Their idea that you would be better off in a "home" while they didn't even know you made me angry. They don't understand you, and because of that, they'll never be able to fully understand me, because you are a part of who I am.

I swallowed the comment of a friend who said they always kinda thought of us as Dad, Mom, Jenny, Rachel, *and their dog, Ben*. I know they didn't mean it to hurt me, but it still stung.

I remember the launching of "Ben's Buddies" at church, in hopes of finding some friends for you. Months went by, and nobody called to take you out for ice cream, or a movie, or just to hang out. But they always let us know when they saw us that they were "still planning on it, but have just been so busy lately."

The problem was that you were the one who wasn't busy; that was the whole point of Ben's Buddies! Any night of the week was wide open for you, and it didn't seem fair that you couldn't go have fun with friends as I could just because people were too "busy." Your stubborn anticipation for them to come through on their promises is an example to me.

I don't say all this to get back at the people who've hurt you. I'm not angry with them, just sad. They've missed out on a wonderful relationship they could have had with you. Some of them *have* changed and started pursuing your friendship. I can't describe how happy it makes me when people discover you! To see you smiling your goodbyes after a night at a friend's house is one of the most wonderful things I know.

You probably won't get to read this letter while we're on earth, although we're praying for your healing yet. But I hope that other sisters and brothers with someone like you in their family will be encouraged by it. We all feel alone sometimes, and it's nice to know that someone else feels the same way we do. I also hope that other people will be challenged to seek out the lonely, the different, and the hurting. That's who Jesus hung out with. Isn't he great?

Thank you for being happy with how God made you. Just Ben. I love you the way you are.

Love forever,
Jen

CHAPTER 12

Becoming a Man—Together

Big and tall, yet oh so small

Many cultures have rituals and traditions that usher their sons into adulthood. It seems that eighteen is a magical number in the United States: that enchanted time when most young men graduate from high school, sign up for military service, plan for college, or begin training for their chosen profession. Often, proud parents rattle off achievements, goals, and dreams for their sons stepping over that invisible threshold into manhood.

We celebrated that passage of our firstborn son a little differently, as many parents of special needs children do. I began filling out paperwork for his first income check—from the Social Security Administration—about a month before his birthday. We opened a checking account he would never understand and never sign for. Reports from speech, occupational and physical therapists; notes from the behavioral psychologist; and records from teachers filled our mailbox in preparation for his yearly individual educational planning meeting. (The IEP is a plan developed each year for special education students in conjunction with their parents and all the specialists or interested parties in their life.)

"Ben will stay on a chosen task for 10 minutes … He can trace simple lines and stays in-between two lines going from point A to point B. When asked to draw a person, Ben draws a face (circle) with what I'm sure are eyes, mouth, and maybe a nose, but they are not in their place. When asked to write, he scribbles, seldom going off the page …"

I sat staring at the papers. Nothing new. How many reports had I read over the years, saying virtually the same thing in different ways? "Planning meeting." *Huh! What can we plan? What goals are even possible?*

"Ben can point to most body parts when asked slowly and sometimes repeatedly. Ben does not like to do work. When we ask him, he pouts and lately has either pounded fists on the table or given us 'the fist' … His school assessments have consistently identified him as developmentally delayed with an IQ in the low twenties and an impairment description of *Severely Mentally Impaired*. He functions at a preschool level with most abilities being in the chronological age of two to four."

Sighing, I laid the paper down. Gently, God spoke peace into my heart again with a familiar verse: "See, I have engraved you on the palms of my hands;" Isaiah 49:16a

I made him. I love him. I love you! *All right, God*, I thought. *You see things that can't be measured. I know that. But Lord, I can only do this if we do it together.*

Ben joined me at that pre-eighteenth birthday IEPC (individualized educational planning committee) meeting. It was his first time at the official meeting. He drew faces with a gift of a pen from his party-loving principal, always finding special ways to celebrate hard and important things. Ben's team (the professionals in his life, plus me) talked guardedly about his attitude, his handsome, beautiful smile, and … his behavioral problems. We left out trigger words like *timeout*, *pulling hair*, *attacks*, and *biting* with Ben in the room. We changed some goals for the next year. Then, together, we signed the papers—he, carefully, with his distinctive "B."

"Adulthood" and all that it meant was too much for the two-to-four-year-old brain inside that six feet, two inch, two-hundred-pound body! My husband and I often lay awake wondering what had happened to our smiling, dimpled boy. Calls, emails, and letters from the school came as fast and furious as Ben's increasingly hostile moods. The first ring of the phone made me feel anxious and sick.

Ben's attacks—on a teacher, an aide, a bus driver, a small boy—became daily occurrences. Often, I was called to come and drive him home because he wasn't safe on the bus. Tears coursed down my face as I read a written report detailing every moment of Ben's attack on a substitute bus driver—repeatedly, wildly!

Ben's tears and remorse usually followed these episodes. We were all miserable together. These outbursts had been rare and almost manageable up to that point, though I know Ben's siblings had taken much more abuse from him than they revealed to us. Now they were no longer safe in our home when Ben was around. I wondered how badly he could hurt someone with the superhuman strength he exhibited at those times. But, I quickly dismissed those thoughts as *disloyal,* wrong! I was angry at my shame. I gained a whole new empathy for parents of wayward children, or those having run-ins with the police.

Ben's behaviors had blown way out of control. Our last solution, so he would be allowed to continue riding the bus, was to strap him into an industrial-style shoulder and waist harness each morning, like a dangerous animal. We unbuckled him from it each night. Only under restraint could he ride the bus to school and back.

We began the pharmaceutical journey that has continued to this day, and will very probably continue for Ben's whole life. After two unsuccessful tries, and several scary months in this strange new world, we found the right medication—we thought. Ben was diagnosed first with schizophrenia, which was changed to bipolar mood disorder along with severe separation anxiety. That process of medicating for that evolving diagnosis would take much longer, and included an added diagnosis of severe attachment mood disorder.

In Michigan, when someone with developmental delays turns eighteen, parents must file for legal guardianship or appoint another legal guardian. Otherwise, the eighteen-year-old automatically becomes a ward of the state. We started the filing process, and a formal hearing was set.

Ed, Ben, and I walked into the old brick courthouse, stood at the groaning elevator, and watched law enforcement officers and handcuffed individuals arriving for their hour in court. We stood for a bit in the hallway before we were ushered into the judge's chambers together. Smiling, Ben's attorney welcomed him and asked him to sit directly in front of the judge's bench. We were shown seats behind the rail. We gave Ben lots of smiles and thumbs-up, praying he wouldn't have an incident right there.

The judge asked me to please rise and take the stand. (Then I prayed **I** wouldn't have an incident in court!) I raised my right hand and swore to "tell the whole truth and nothing but the truth, so help me God."

Yes, we wanted to become Ben's legal guardians.

Yes, we promised to do the best we could for him.

Inwardly I screamed, *haven't we been doing that for eighteen years of sleepless nights, bedwetting, therapies, educational meetings, phone calls, canceled plans, ruined dreams, and tears?*

The judge thanked me and said I could sit down. Then he questioned Ben's caseworker.

"What would you say his mental abilities are? In your opinion, will they ever change?" Tapping his pen against his computer screen, eager to get to the end of his day, the judge wanted a concise answer.

"No, your honor, his mental ability will remain between two to four years of age. That will not change."

The judge then addressed Ben, telling him his rights. Ben, of course, understood nothing. He turned around repeatedly to be reassured by us, smiling warily. I knew it was just a formality. But the cold list of black-and-white facts and the magnitude of Ben's lifetime needs, along with the responsibilities we were agreeing to, bore down on me like a leaden gavel. I fought my emotions, but tears had surfaced and would not stop.

The black-robed personage asked Ben if he agreed to the guardianship as it stood. *Don't go crazy now, Ben!* He continued to smile and turned to look at us again, puzzled by my tears. I grinned and waved assurance I didn't feel.

The judge leafed through his papers. An electronic recorder received his verdict. "Let it be noted," he droned in his five o'clock voice, "that he did not respond."

"No!" I nearly screamed. *He cannot respond in words until we open our eyes in heaven. Do you have any idea of what that means for us? For him?* But a judge's job is one of facts and signatures, not feelings and emotions.

We were ushered from the courtroom then, wearing our new title: legal guardians. The title "Ben's parents" was no longer enough. We were now Ben's *legal* voice.

As we were walking out to the parking lot, Ben's attorney reminded us of the many families who break up over the stress of raising a child like Ben, and how good it was that Ben had such a stable family. Ed and I squeezed each other's hands, knowing what we had promised. We then drove home in silence, all three of us, still together.

Man of Three

Happily pushing a cart for me, eagerly signing, "Ice cream, please!"
When did you get to be a man full-grown, toddling through the store?

How do we protect a man of three decades, or explain him to the ignorant?
Still and always a little boy. Impulsive. Inquisitive. Handsome, see?

Smiling through the baby years, your smile now given to those who care.
Answering a bullfrog, you wait for its reply. Cooing at a child, you wonder why they run.

You're big and tall, yet oh so small. No words developed as you grew.
You speak, instead, with all your heart. My beautiful, brave boy Ben.

Surely an athlete, positively a star—a man beyond all men, thought Dad.
Living large, with eyes free of judgment; wise, wise teacher, that's who you are.

CHAPTER 13

Doors to Manhood

Secretly, joyfully, I smile at their shame

Soon after Ben's eighteenth birthday, another rite of passage—the school prom invitation—came home in his backpack. The prom was held every year, regardless of age, but I had never taken Ben.

That school bag carried a binder with a running dialogue between his teacher or aides and me. I read or wrote in it each day to exchange awareness of behaviors or school happenings. It carried the words Ben did not have.

When I opened the very formal invitation, the theme "Amethyst Elegance" piqued my interest. It sounded like an excellent way for Ben and I to make a happy memory together. As usual, I was a little starry-eyed and a lot naive.

Thousands of small white lights romanced the school gym when we walked through the giant metal doors on prom night. White Grecian pillars were draped in soft purple silk, and white tulle encircled with twinkling lights invited everyone to step onto the dance floor. A mirrored ball hung overhead, reflecting dancing colored lights and repelling all thoughts of "behaviors" and "violence."

Principal Sue competed with herself at every banquet. Each year's offering was more elaborate than the year before. This year was no different. Circular, linen-covered tables were candlelit and set with sparkling dinnerware. The mood was soft and dreamy. A fantastic aroma swirled in from the kitchen, filling the gymnasium-turned-ballroom.

Ben's mood? Tense and alert. We tried all through dinner to keep him calm. His family of teachers and I gave him lots of thumbs-up signs, hoping to attract him to a meal that, under other circumstances, we knew he'd love. His crisis team stayed nearby. Our eyes met knowingly, monitoring his level of anxiety, all of us together grieving the smiling boy who seemed more and more lost to us. Ready or not, prom night.

I didn't even think about what I would wear until that day. I decided on a long skirt with a matching short jacket. Getting Ben fitted for a tux was out of the question during those difficult days. Dad's sports coat worked. His sisters had fussed over my hair and oohed and aahed over Ben's dimples.

Ben's style of dancing is more of a broad hip arc with posterior swinging than feet shuffling. His hands end up in the air, sometimes clapping, but often just hanging out there—perhaps opening and closing, depending on his level of concentration. A high-pitched, squealing "Yah!" usually escapes. He gives high-fives to his partner and others while he happily bumps everyone around him.

But Ben wasn't happy that night. In fact, he grew more distressed as his friends boogied closer and taunted, "Ben! Look at me!" or "I'm gonna dance wit' yo' mama!"

I was hoping to dance away some of the pain of recent months that evening. I mentally celebrated the milestones we'd passed over the last eighteen years. I enjoyed the simplicity of Ben's special friends at this school. We had known them since we moved nearby four years prior. It was an excellent school for the developmentally disabled—the *severely* and *profoundly* developmentally disabled. I laughed with the other students at their wild dances, wheelchair moves, and childlike flirtation.

"Will you marry me?"

"You're Ben's mom."

"Yup, I am. Doesn't he look handsome?"

"Ben makes me scared!" several said, backing away. "He has to be good."

"Yes," I choked out, "he's trying real hard!"

I realized I'd been dancing with a younger version of this "scary" man, one whose dimples and hugs charmed everyone. Right about then, before we were halfway through the night, Ben tore my arm away. His wild eyes no longer resembled those of my beloved son. He gave a terrible, shrieking howl, and I heard—and felt—the palm of his hand slapping my face.

As the shock wore off, the verse I'd claimed his whole life mocked me: "…I have engraved you on the palms of my hands." Isaiah 49:16a (NIV)

Was God blind? Deaf? Was he mute too?

Ben's steady sobbing, "Mama! Mama!" and penitent tears showed his confusion and how sorry he was. But I didn't know the young man his teacher and aides were holding down at the side of the room. My tears flowed uncontrollably. "Yes, Ben, Momma forgives you. You're okay!" I assured him as we waited for him (and his mom) to calm down enough for the ride home.

As I lay in Ed's arms later that night, we quietly rehearsed what we were about to do, knowing it would alter Ben's life—and ours—forever. It was no longer a future, desperate option. It had morphed into a present plan of action. Beginning at the courthouse, we had walked through the door to Ben's future.

We had listened in horror as our younger children described locking the doors of their rooms to escape Ben's violence. His older sister—his protector, Jenny—reluctantly confirmed that he'd attacked her recently too, pulling her hair while she was driving, with the two younger children in the car! We knew Ben couldn't help what was happening, but he could no longer safely live in our home. Ed and I began searching for an adult foster care home.

I'm so grateful I have memories of happier days—lots of them. Days like the one when I wrote this poem, for instance.

Ah-Yah-Yah-Muh!

Proudly he pedals down the street, ding-dinging the tiny bell
Greeting strangers like his dearest friends
His "thank you"—hand touched to the mouth—
A kiss, sincerely meant, given though others soon forget
The bike is small for his oversize body—this man, but yet a child

Miniscule goals his report cards reveal
Distinguishing a quarter from a dime
Or finishing the *E*, then *N*, behind *B*; no alphabet learning for Ben
Signing some concepts, and *Mama* and *Dah*
He manages a nearly wordless life

Peacefully rocking on the porch swing
Teenage boys point from their car
Waving a friendly response, he yells a raucous "Hahee!"
Startled by his lack of intimidation, they catch themselves waving
Secretly, joyfully, I smile at their shame

Helping him brush his teeth, fixing his reckless dressing
We shave his very grown-up chin; toddler mistakes we clean
He sets the table all askew while
Clapping for his big achievement
We praise and thank him for his help; our big boy, only three

Pulling the blanket over his six-foot frame
He responds with his longest sentence
"Ah-yah-yah-muh!" then chuckling, grins … and puckers for a kiss
Kissing his heavily whiskered cheek, I tuck in his favorite bear
"Thank you, Ben! I love you too."

Three months after the prom, there was an opening. It was not in a home we would have chosen, but there were no options. We knew virtually nothing about adult foster care. Finding one for a person with such extreme behaviors severely limited our options.

We walked through the windowless door of the brick, ranch-style home with Ben—just a few city blocks from his school. He repeatedly signed "No." He did not want to spend a moment there. We had begun talking to him about a new house some time before, knowing he would never truly understand, but hoping we could somehow prepare him for the day he would have to stay behind another door. That talk only made him nervous. Severe Separation Anxiety is a real disorder; he was suffering.

One late-summer afternoon, Ben entered my office, smiling tentatively at me and signing "house." I called him over to my chair and said softly, "Ben, when you go to your new house, I want you to remember how much Momma loves you!"

I felt myself flinch as he leaned over … but gently he took a pen and opened my hand in his. Carefully, precisely, he wrote the letter *B*. My tears brimmed over as Ben "engraved" his name on my palm. I lifted my hand and held it to my heart, telling Ben how much I loved him. How much I would always love him.

That night, our family took a ride to the Lake Michigan channel where we'd made some great memories over the last four years. Walking and quietly talking, we knew this would be the last time we were all together before life changed for us. Ducks and sailboats passing through the channel looked enviably carefree.

Ben and I fell behind the others; he was afraid of the height and the strangeness of the path. I took his hand, and we ambled down the pier together, waves swelling on either side.

Jen, our gentle-spirited firstborn, would soon be moving into a mobile home—her first *apartment.* She and Ben would leave our home within a month of each other. Yes, we would all be together again, but not ever in the same way.

Ed and I believed we'd done all we could do. Ready or not, manhood had arrived for Ben. He would have to start holding other hands that would lead him down new, very rocky paths. Jen would be walking some scary paths also as a young woman on her own for the first time.

The seven of us completed our walk without the usual banter, all remembering happier times. Then we piled into the old station wagon. *Now what? Now where?*

Slowly, Ed drove back past our farm and into our little town, purposefully finding the familiar path to the ice cream shop so we could celebrate this moment with *family*—together.

Seventeen-plus years later, I'm happy to say Ben found his smile and good humor again, and still loves to draw. His drawings are usually smiley faces. But we will never forget the years when he lost that beautiful smile, and we didn't know if it would return.

I have no idea what Ben was thinking about when he drew this picture, but it started me thinking about big, rectangular objects made of wood, metal, or glass: bedroom doors, bathroom doors, and glass sliding doors, just to name a few. I am making a conscious decision to leave car doors off the list at this time!

Many years ago, in our first little house, we jumped awake to someone knocking in the middle of the night. Cautiously, we made our way through the dimly lit hallway to the dining-room patio door. How long he'd been there, we didn't know, but we found Ben outside, on the cement patio. He had switched on the floodlight and tried to catch the millers flying toward the bulb. When they landed on the glass, he would execute them. He wasn't yet eight years old but—like some two-year-olds—he liked John the Baptist's grasshopper diet. Lockdown in his room was immediate!

The unique door marked "boys" or "girls" became an interesting choice for Ben's adolescent and teen years. I was often the parent with him in those years before the Americans with Disabilities Act of 1990 and ADA's fabulous creation, the "family" bathroom. We trod some awkward ground before that date, and many times after when there were still no options.

Ben always needed help in the bathroom, but he had no safety parameters in his brain. So when we were in a busy place, and Ben was no longer welcome in the women's side, I would send him into the men's room, knowing he was old enough to at least do what he was supposed to do. Then I would ask men who were coming out, "Is the young man doing okay in there?" I received stares and some interesting comments, meanwhile praying he wasn't greeting anyone with his signature "best bud" hug as he came out of a stall!

Ed had an entertaining experience when we were camping out west. Ben was about thirteen years old, getting tall and lanky. The campground bathroom was pretty dark inside, with no lights on and limited daylight coming in. As Ed was helping Ben—not quite out of the stall—a young boy opened the door, not seeing them at first. Ben eagerly hollered his *very* friendly "Hahee!" from the darkness. That poor little guy gave a yell and left a spotty trail in the sandy cement, running away as fast as he could.

Remember, I said we locked his bedroom door? He found out how to open it. Waking or asleep, our ears stayed tuned to a couple of sounds during those years. One came from the tiny apartment-sized stove: specifically the cranking of its electrical knobs. The other was the sound of the old TV knob as channels were changed. There was also another door that was appealing to Ben, but it did not make a noticeable noise—the door on the refrigerator.

In the dead of night, around one of his early birthdays, Ben decided to set up a party for us. When we awoke to the smell of something burning, we found the cook preparing a birthday feast to share. He had poured oatmeal onto the stove, missing the pan he'd placed there. More than one electric burner was red-hot. On the counter were four or five dishes full of Jell-O, hand served from the fridge.

I'm convinced that though we rarely got six hours of sleep without interruption, the angels had to be swarming the house, stationed and ready for that random hour when our bodies would surrender to sleep. Being awakened by Ben could only be likened to the terror of a fire alarm going off in the dead of night. You knew he was up, but you couldn't see how far you were behind him!

A few years later, we were awakened by a literal alarm, immediately catching the unmistakable odor of smoke! By then, we were in a much larger home, and discovered a whimpering Ben in the family room, with evidence of three separate burns in the carpet! Thankfully, there was fire retardant in the rug. We were grateful he hadn't ignited something that would have been explosive or worse.

Sleuthing his trail, we discovered Ben had gotten out of the bedroom again, and started paper towels on fire at the electric stove. He probably walked ten to twelve feet with them burning, on his way to the fireplace. But he dropped them in the family room. Thankfully, he hadn't been burned. Those pyromaniacal years ended soon after that, and we were grateful our insurance covered repair of the escapee's crime.

Then there's the infamous story of the Boston cream pie, bought for a special occasion, waiting behind the refrigerator door! When we awoke that morning, the only evidence was the empty container behind the shut refrigerator door. Ben had found a way out of his locked bedroom again.

The big yellow bus door has an almost sacred place in our memories. Ben's last driver was Stephanie—with a giant smile and a warm, quick laugh. Her giggling fall backward into Ben's lap when he shot her with his finger-pointing pistol was typically met with his own wild, surprised giggle. We had a pretty steady tradition of placing Ben on that bus, decorated for each season with window decals and colorful characters. Standing outside—or under the porch roof if it was raining or snowing—we waved goodbye. Ben would inevitably shoot us with his imaginary pistol. We would shoot him back, laughing, often running after the bus like we were going to "get him." That never ceased to make him giggle and gasp! We blew kisses and waved until he was out of sight.

The morning of September 4, 2001 was unlike anything we had ever experienced. We helped Ben get showered and dressed for school, Ed shaved his whiskers and brushed his teeth, and we opened the door and walked outside, where the maples were just starting to turn yellow. Stephanie pushed open the squeaky door leading up to her cheerfully decorated domain, acting like it was just a regular day. But we could see her pain when she shared a glance after she had hooked him up in his seat. She knew the plan for that day; it was to be Ben's last ride on her bus.

When Stephanie smiled her sad goodbye and closed that big metal door, we all knew we were ending an era, and that day would end very badly. Ed and I stood with arms locked as we began the usual farewell routine. "We love you, Ben," we choked out. But as soon as the big yellow bus lurched out of our driveway, we slumped in each other's arms, barely able to breathe. Sixteen years' worth of almost year-around school days ended right there.

That evening, Ben would be strapped into another, smaller van—one he would fight against entering every day. Instead of coming home, he would be chauffeured to his new home. He was accompanied by someone he knew and trusted, but- as his parents—we could not see him for at least two weeks. The intention was to try to sever the bond that had held us together through the last eighteen years and help him get used to a new routine—he with Separation Anxiety Disorder.

The closed, locked doors at that first adult foster care home were part of our nightmares for four long years. We didn't know anything about adult foster care, but we had been desperate, needing protection for Ben's siblings and us. When we toured the only home available, they explained something about fire rules, which purportedly stated that all doors must remain locked inside the house. That included all the bedrooms and the office. They also said the windows could not be locked for fire safety reasons.

Ben tried to escape frequently. Staff there once reported that he climbed out of the window, but when he found out he had no place to go, he ended up knocking on the front door in the middle of the night. That scared the staff out of their inattention, I'm sure!

After four years and four formal complaints to the state about conditions at that house, a new AFC home opened for Ben. The first thing that caught our attention about the new house was that the blinds weren't pulled tight at all hours of the day. The door was unlocked; an automatic chime noted entrances and exits. When we took a tour, we were thrilled to see all the bedroom and office doors flung wide open. The seemingly happy men freely moved about the whole house. The friendly manager told us this house was *their* home. Nothing was locked except for medications and potentially dangerous items.

That particular door opened a whole new life for Ben. The freedom he felt there, and the respect he was given, brought tremendous joy to Ben … and to his famiy!

CHAPTER 14

Dah, Ben, and More

That would take a lot of fiber

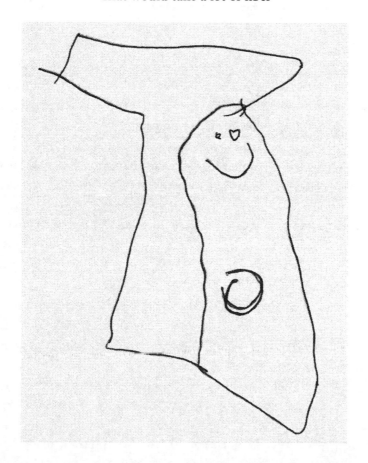

We now have a darling grandson, Vinny—short for Kelvin, the name he shares with his daddy. Vinny is walking now, but for many months his mama, Jen, would tell him he was "tall as a tree" when she was snuggling with him. He got into that, and still pushes his fists into the air when you remind him how tall he is. When Vinny gives an eager hug to Grandpa now, Grandpa whispers, "Car parts," in his ear. (Guess who's trying to influence a two-year-old?)

Ben's dad is just short of six feet, three inches tall, and, I think, was much like a tree to the younger Ben (and probably now to Vinny). Notice the twinkle of the heart-shaped eye in this drawing? It's a fun depiction of the extraordinary love between Ben and his dad. Ben spent hours—possibly accumulated years—on Ed's lap as he was growing up. Right through Ben's teen years, his dad was his refuge from all that was too hard and too confusing. Dad was also protection *from* Ben himself in strange, uncomfortable situations, keeping Ben from reacting in ways that could cause damage to himself or others.

We came to believe, over the years, that Ben was for us "the least of these" that Jesus referenced in Matthew 25:40 (NIV). We don't always rise to that challenge, but we remind ourselves to treat Ben as if he were Jesus in our home. His love for us is breathtaking at times. He is a precious gift, and Ed takes great delight in being Ben's dad. Ed has brushed Ben's very adult teeth, shaved him, and wrestled with him.

During most visits home from AFC those first years, I would find Ben wrapped in Ed's arms at some point. They would sit on the couch, watching a video of Ben's childhood—all the family together, as we once were. That represented Ben's happiest memories, I think. His obsession with that video is gone now, and thankfully, he's happy in his home.

Ben often pulls us into a game of peekaboo, hiding behind one of our trees or just covering his eyes with his hands. Frequently he shuffles his tall frame behind one of his lean sisters with a big, conspiratorial grin on his face. "Where's Ben?" we ask. "Oh, *there* he is!" we exclaim as he giggles and magically reappears.

We used to play peekaboo by phone too. After Ed went through his Donald Duck imitation and some verbal play, Ben would become very silent. We would ask, "Where's Ben?"

He would make us ask a couple of times, but always we heard that big, booming "Buh!" at the end.

Security for Ben has changed very much. Ed was always the tree for Ben to hide behind when life got scary. Ben now has to rely on others for safety and protection. But when he is with us, it's often Dad's hand that he reaches for. Ed is still the tree Ben hides behind. Ed has always taken his position as protector very seriously.

When Ben began adult foster care, we were not supposed to see him for at least two weeks, to give him time to adjust to the new norm. He was terrified, of course, and went ballistic in that house of strangers.

His new caregivers made a terrible decision. Their van appeared in our driveway less than twenty-four hours after that fateful day when he entered that first AFC home. Ben was wildly scared, desperately fighting the strangers. Now his trusted protector, Ed, had to force him back into that van.

"We love you, Ben," Ed kept repeating through his tears and gritted teeth, "but you have to stay in your new home." Ben's screams and clawing haunted Ed for years to come. The fact that the 9/11 terrorist attack happened one week after he was placed in foster care gives you an idea of the despair we were feeling through those terrible days in our beloved country.

Sadly, that scene would be repeated many times in the next four years, whenever we brought Ben home for a visit and made the return trip to that horror house. Grace has helped us all live beyond those memories of painful, desperate battles as Ben tried to climb back into our car. The memory of him standing in that quiet residential street will never leave us. Ben's wailing as we drove away was an incredible challenge to Ed.

Years before Ben was born, Ed shared a conversation with our realtor. We were looking at the house we planned to buy—specifically the spare room above the garage. Ed observed that it would be a great place if you had a child with special needs. The realtor replied, "That would take a lot of fiber." Of course, he wasn't talking about the kind touted on cereal boxes! He meant the moral fiber that would be needed to sustain that sort of sacrifice.

Ed, of course, didn't think of that statement until years later. He mentioned it when we were talking about the physical, mental, spiritual, and emotional strain that we had experienced over the years.

I am always conscious of other parents going through painful times, sometimes for years, feeling helpless and all alone. Sometimes there are terribly complex situations with few—if any—options. I want to remind you to knock down every door and find out what scenarios are possible … and keep asking! Then let God do the impossible.

We prayed often, and Ben's happiness today is only because of God's grace. That grace opened a lot of doors for Ben, and the MOKA Foundation[7] is one of them.

There will likely be more rough spots ahead too, but we are grateful for every measure of grace along this trip. It is one beautiful part of our story. I've talked a lot about God's healing power and what that has meant for my family. We've come to understand that without Ben and all that he is, we probably would not have grown in our relationship with Ben's Creator as we have. We've been highly blessed to have Ben as a teacher and beloved son and brother in our home.

On one vacation when Ben was about seven years old, Ed went fishing. That summer day he watched as another man started fishing with his son, smaller and younger than Ben. The boy talked with his dad like a little man. It affected Ed profoundly. His shoulders were stooped and his eyes red when he returned. Quietly, he said, "it's interesting having a son like Ben."

Five years after that summer vacation, we were ecstatic about the pending birth of our last

---

[7] MOKA Foundation, From their website:http://www.moka.org/specialized-residential

child, a son. When Ed found out we were expecting a boy, he pledged to me that *no one* would *ever* "replace" Ben. James Matthew didn't replace Ben, but he brought great joy—in his quiet, thoughtful responses, his gift of humor, bright mind, and his athletic build and interests. His personality is very much like Ed's, and they have a great relationship, enjoying a love of muscle cars, especially. Ben's younger brother has become his "big brother" now, and—Ben would be so jealous—James gets to shoot real guns on the range as a soldier in the US Army, standing six feet, eight inches tall!

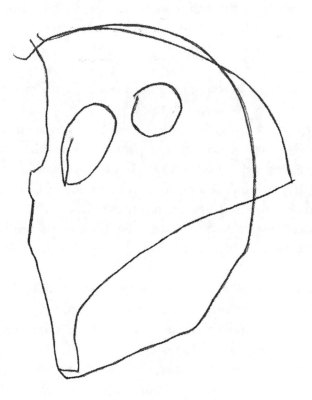

Many of our feelings could not be articulated back when Ben was small. But some time ago I found these scribbled thoughts from Ed on a notebook page—one Ben subsequently used for a drawing. The wrenching sadness of the character echoes the pain of the questions Ed voiced:

> Ben is the least of these.
> The man with the most faith may be just approaching the faith of a little child.
> Would I have Ben healed? The pain produces growth.
> Do you stop the growth?

The big questions of life don't always have answers. We grow through them, just as we open doors only when we come to them. Ben does a great job of making us all laugh along the journey.

When I show Ben family pictures on my phone, he wiggles his tongue and tickles the screen. When he uses Skype or Facetime with Jen's family, he giggles excitedly. Little Vinny yells to Uncle Ben, making sure his voice is heard over that of his big sister Ana.

When Dreams Seem to Die

They only die for an instant,
But it really feels like a long time.
And it's not easy.

Dreams don't always die,
They can change.

The caterpillar dreams of green leaves,
Butterflies dream of light, flight, and flowers
Lives are like leaves. In due time they show forth,
Eager to begin singing and working.

But alas, some never unfurl. Others become damaged.
Hurt, they soldier on as strength allows, and fall too soon.
Most last the season,
And from an optimistic vantage point, look full and bright.

But all will fall.

They grow tired and gravity gently lowers them
To join all other tribes and nations of leaves.
We too, likewise.

But ah, not so fast.
For God's children, the soul and the dreams in pregnant silence remain.
Then, with a grand crescendo that earthquakes through our core,
We will see Jesus, and Benjamin— the son of my right hand—
Singing a new song together, strong and hearty victors,
Joined with champions from all tribes and nations!

All aspirations met.
Satisfied.

CHAPTER 15

From the Heart

No teeth to brush except my own!

I unearthed a journal from 2001 during a recent move. One of the first entries was written the day we sent Ben to a new home after school. He had no understanding of what was happening, even though we did as much as we could to prepare him. We took him to visit a couple of times beforehand. He, of course, cried and resisted each time, but he didn't have any real knowledge of what was ahead of him. We brought his favorite chair, his bed, and some toys there during the school day.

September 4, Tuesday

Put him on the bus today. "Fifteen years," Ed said. Fifteen years of bus rides for Ben. After we talked to Stephanie, they left. Ed and I cried in each other's arms. He will miss his buddy. We will miss him! God help us all. The Jabez prayer (enlarge my territory; bless him) is a good prayer for Ben too. Last night when I opened my Bible, it opened naturally to Isaiah 42:16 (NIV) with no bookmark. "Praise you, Lord, that you will lead him and protect him! Along unfamiliar paths, you will guide him. You'll turn this darkness into light and make the rough places smooth. You will do it. You will not forsake him!"

September 6, 3:15 a.m.

Lying awake—Ben.
How many years—Ben.
Wet beds and wet body—Ben.
Eighteen and a half years of your wakefulness.
Now you're finally in someone else's care
but still you wake us.
It's impossible to sleep
Knowing you're there
Knowing you're scared—Ben.
God help me, I miss him so—
His hugs, his kisses
his eager-eyed, jumping-up-and-down exclamations
His wet pucker and his
so-eager-to-see-me toddler run.
God help us through these empty days!
No struggling to make you stand still for shaving
No teeth to brush except my own
No bus in the driveway
At ten minutes till seven
No nighttime's soiled laundry to greet me—Ben.

—•◆•—

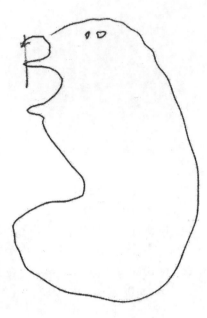

This peculiar caricature isn't as amusing to me as it might seem to the average person. It has always reminded me of a terrifying movie where a fiendish creature envelops and destroys a town. In this case, that living amoeba threatens to engulf our Ben ("B"). The names and shapes that the monsters take vary, but all are devastating to Ben. Some of my readers may know precisely what I mean, as the monster of some diagnosis envelopes their loved one.

I first thought of this drawing as a stifled scream. Our Ben, who was often sweet, tender, and caring, could be swallowed up by the bipolar bear, making him strike out at unsuspecting friends, staff, and family members. His personality, and ultimately his very self, would be lost for a time.

Ben drew this figure in the fall of 2004, three years after entering adult foster care. When he came home for a night or two, he often let out a heart-wrenching sob as I tucked him in. He has never known how to camouflage his emotions. The rawness of his longing seemed to suck all the air out of the room, preventing his mouth from closing, filling his eyes—and mine—with tears. Nothing could assuage that desolate lament.

His longing for what he once knew and his hunger for home would crush him at that moment. My mother's heart wanted to protect him, to take him back home, regardless of what we would all suffer—regardless if it would indeed make him happy or not. Anything to stop the nightmare!

We ended the overnights altogether when we realized they were prolonging his adjustment and causing far too much pain. It was time for me to make the final cut to the umbilical cord.

There would be one more year in a place we knew to be inadequate and possibly dangerous for Ben, but we had no options. He stayed and we prayed, shortening our visits to a few hours every other week.

Now, over a decade later, Ben is usually pleased to go to his home, a much, much happier place than that first miserable one. It's almost impossible to describe how wonderful that is. But he still battles severe attachment disorder—the other demon—which varies in its turbulence.

The leviathan of severe developmental delays is the most significant beast Ben contends with. A brain that would be okay for a one-year-old or, possibly, two-year-old boy is grossly inadequate for a man in his thirtieth year.

I don't spend time questioning anymore, though. I *know* that God is watching over Ben, more fiercely protective, more loving than I could ever be. God is far greater than any diagnosis that Ben experiences. Monsters—real or imagined—are always more menacing in the dark. We worship a loving Father who sheds light on our path. Morning light brings fresh mercy, grace, and peace for this momma.

In reality, things began to normalize for the children at home, when Ben left the house. For Ed and me, too. It took a while, but we realized our bodies had been in a constant state of alert when Ben was present, ready to respond to anything. It was not healthy. Regular conversations with our other kids were often abbreviated, and their needs usually came second.

Sometimes it seemed there were no choices. Other times it felt as if we didn't have any power over anything! In the end, we believe Ben positively affected the lives of all our children. Sometimes he made them stronger. In other ways, I wish we could do it all over again, only knowing ahead of time how much Ben and Ben's needs would dominate and overshadow their life, so that we could figure out a way to make sure his siblings were getting our attention, and that they weren't bearing the burden of his care. I believe many needs of our other children—probably especially the two siblings closet to Ben, in age—went unmet.

I've listed several articles here (some as recent as this publication year), regarding Special Needs Siblings' struggles. They are valuable reading for every parent, and for every adult sibling of a special needs person.

Endnotes

Jamie Davis Smith, on Parenting. "Eight things siblings of special needs children struggle with", December 20, 2016, https://www.washingtonpost.com/news/parenting/wp/2016/12/20/8-things-siblings-of-children-with-special-needs-struggle-with/?noredirect=on&utm_term=.39bf8518adcf

Lisa Jamieson, "Unsung Heroes: Special-Needs Heroes", January 9, 2018, http://www.keyministry.org/church4everychild/2 018/1/9/unsung-heroes-special-needs-siblings

Jeanne Gowen Dennis, "Siblings needs when you have a special needs child",2009, Focus on the Family, Canada, https://www.focusonthefamily.ca/content/siblings-needs-when-you-have-a-special -needs-child

CHAPTER 16

Olympians!

Let me be brave in the attempt

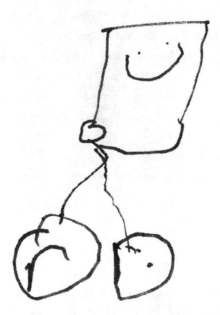

The little heart-shaped hand of this character makes me smile, but the happy square-headed face is fantastic. The feet are adorable but, as you can imagine, entirely unfit for sports. This drawing has always reminded me of Ben and his Special Olympics stint in cross-country skiing.

Everything about cross-country skiing was fun for Ben! He giggled when he tried to walk while training in carpeted hallways. He repeatedly fell, laughing hysterically, because the skis crossed one another, following the lead of his left foot, which curved in. Later he would have corrective surgery, but by then he had already eliminated cross-country skiing from his "most favorite" list. The surgery didn't help on a long term basis.

Eunice Kennedy Shriver founded Special Olympics, and I believe Martha Katt took Mrs. Shriver's passion seriously! Martha was the nurse at the Ottawa Area Center, where Ben went to school, and I think she was also the director of our Area 12 Special Olympics in Michigan for a time. I'm grateful for Martha's endless hours contributing to our children's health and success. If you spent any time researching or listening to the speeches of Mrs. Shriver, you could not help but be inspired too. She worked tirelessly to change stigmas and perceptions for all persons with mental and physical disabilities.

We tried a lot of sports. I remember a few sessions of soccer training that we participated in for a month or so. Ben giggled uncontrollably and ran after every loose ball, in *every* direction. We decided he would need to learn some directional skills before messing up everyone else's earnest play!

If you have ever participated in Special Olympics events, you know that speed is not the order of the day. Just trying to get a bunch of free-spirited athletes into one area took quite a bit of manipulation and reboots. Did I say "boots"? That's a whole other story!

First, we met up with our group of athletes. Then we met the volunteer helper for our athlete— one of many young persons with an eager, but frightened look in their eyes. Next, we figured out where the events were going to be, hurrying to the warming shack every chance we got on that freezing winter day. All in all, we stayed quite busy that morning.

Behind the shed, on a level area, a microphone and loudspeaker were set up, with the American flag flying. After a few words of direction, a young girl on an incline was handed something like a torch. She was fully practiced and ready. Her tongue worked furiously over her chapped lips. Amid the eager acknowledgment of the appreciative crowd, she was reminded several times that she was holding *fire* in her bright mittens.

The spirit of Greece electrified our pyromaniacal Ben, who immediately asked for the torch— translation: *loudly* grunted and said "please" by rubbing his glove in a circular motion on his chest. With his eyes glazing over, he tried to move toward the flame carrier while pointing to himself. His dad kept a firm grip on him until he settled down. We exhaled once the torch was secured in its permanent position for the day.

Next, someone at the microphone called our attention to the flag. Another athlete stepped up to the podium, placed his hand over his heart, and shouted, "I pledge allegiance to the flag …" Proudly we followed suit, hands over our hearts. Then a blushing, eager athlete was ushered to the microphone to repeat the essential pledge for that day. She smiled nervously at the crowd. Someone held the microphone to her mouth. She leaned into it and began, "Let me win …"

Everyone suddenly hushed. A few voices joined hers: "But if I cannot win" …Tears were now falling from more eyes than mine. … "Let me be brave in the attempt."

One year stands out above most in my memory because it includes an exceptional friend: a young man, Dale, who got out of a warm bed that morning just to cheer on Ben and encourage us.

Dale Frye is a talented illustrator and industrial designer who was working with Ed at Prince Corporation at the time. He was born and raised in Southern California and was entirely averse to Michigan weather! His football-injured knees ached on a typical day, let alone in those frigid temperatures. But Dale came anyway, to encourage one notable Olympian and his family.

As soon as Dale arrived, he launched a snowball fight with our girls and then a wrestling match with Ben. The memory of him covered in snow is a vivid reminder of his gift that day. Knowing how much he hated the cold made his sacrifice all the sweeter.

Between each Special Olympics event, there is a great deal of time spent coaxing participants to the spot for their next event, making doubly sure they have the appropriate equipment and have gotten to know their volunteers. An essential part of that introduction is helping the volunteers get to know their participant. As the competitors prepared, Dale patiently waited. Then he positioned himself alongside the cross-country skiing lanes, while we chatted with other parents and with the more verbal Special Olympians about their long list of wins!

We used that same community hollow for several years. Our Olympians had to "ski" on a carpet several times due to insufficient snowfall. But this particular year, there was plenty of snow. We shielded our eyes from the brilliant sparkles, before the loudspeaker barked Ben's name.

Just getting him to stay upright was the first challenge. Added to the effect from his foot curving in was the combined length of the appendages attached to those long feet. Watching him was a lot like being positioned in the front row at a slapstick routine performed by Laurel and Hardy.

It is never impolite to laugh *with* your athlete, especially since he was having such a great time. It is always miserable etiquette to laugh *at* anyone who is trying their hardest. Some whipped down their lane; others turned aside, more distracted by sideline happenings than the distant finish line. We cheered them all on!

Stamping his feet to stave off frostbite, Dale clapped his heavy gloves. Ben received help from parents, volunteers, and other Olympians who helped him get vertical after each fall. Ben responded with all the Olympic spirit within him, laughing at his own silly antics more loudly with each fall. He reflected "let me be brave in the attempt" with true grace!

I don't remember Ben taking part in cross-country skiing again, but the laughter and the happy spirit of all Special Olympians always inspire us.

CHAPTER 17

The Saints Go Marchin' In

With much theatrical polish

Ben drew this spirited portrayal while sitting in church with us one Sunday, many years ago. I can't help but think the character out front—on the right—is one of the saints he knew well, complete with halo. I see all Ben's friends in this picture sometimes. Some stand out; others are just there—like the top row of "n" repeated over and over—filling up the back rows of his life.

May I take this opportunity to say an enormous thank-you to all the smiling, haloed faces who regularly step up to the plate for the Bens in their lives? You jump over lots of hoops. It takes time, and it also takes eyes. I hope the loving examples of saints mentioned in this story might give readers some creative ideas of how to create *inclusively*!

Ben was around nine or ten years old when I finally realized we needed to spend some time and energy teaching people *about* Ben and *how to* relate or help. I had wrongly assumed that the body of Christ would instinctively know. I had to remember how long it took me to learn about the world of mental and physical challenges as Ben grew.

That's when we started an awareness group in our church. It included a married couple, both in wheelchairs; parents who were losing their previously healthy child to a degenerative disease; and others, as well as Gail from the church staff. With Gail's help, we sent out newsletters explaining our thoughts and needs. We began to teach people how they could be of help, and how they could intercede or pray for us.

The church staff created a video, interviewing each family in the group. After watching that video, many people responded. One young family decided they would take Ben to their home for lunch once in a while on Sunday—a huge commitment. Dave said it was the comment I made about how Jesus said to treat "the least of these" like Jesus in our home, the way my husband Ed taught us to think of Ben. Dave wanted to help his sons learn about that kind of love.

Both of Dave's sons were quiet around Ben but quickly learned his humor. They offered Ben their toys and their property (positively losing a little on *that* deal). They learned Ben's language and graciously put up with his occasional bad behavior. The younger of those two boys became a football and basketball star in high school, but tragically, he was killed in a car accident at sixteen years of age.

We reconnected with that family a few years ago. Dave said he never thought twice about committing to spending time with Ben. In fact, he hadn't even discussed it with his wife Cindy before he blurted out their commitment. (I don't recommend that, guys!) Beautiful saints! Their strong testimony now, after losing their promising young son, inspires us to give God the glory and trust him, regardless of our losses. God makes all things beautiful in his time.

Occupying the back row of "n's" in this picture might be Lloyd and Sharon. They were not active in churchy things, but they were two of many saints who made their time with Ben a priority, setting regular dates to have Ben in their home. It couldn't have been easy, but they never excused themselves when their chosen date arrived. The beam on Ben's face whenever we picked him up indicated everyone had had a great time. I know they're glad they knew Ben. We're so blessed to have known them!

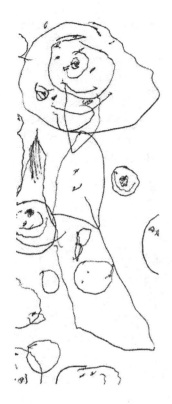

This picture fascinates me. I've enlarged the middle portion here. I know I'm a little strange, but I can see a guy (or maybe several) wearing a tie here. Do you? There's another little face with several eyes and perhaps a big nose inside the big circle. It has an upside-down triangle attached to the bottom, all in the more prominent ring. That could be a little guy with a bit of a tie on the right. And do you see the hint of a halo on his head too?

Well, the more prominent circle represents a bigger head, and there's a double tie on him; Ben put his signature on the bottom part of that tie. This drawing reminds me of several male saints in Ben's life. Two of them were ushers. One always made sure he had a particular peppermint in his pocket for Ben. The other was a favorite because he wore ties that flashed on and off at Christmas or were a little spooky at Halloween. On the Fourth of July—you guessed it: stars and stripes with fireworks. He and Ben were kindred spirits for sure!

Wearing the massive halos are two women, Nicki and Carolyn. They were janitors at our church then, and teachers at the Wednesday night children's club when our first set of children were young. Quietly one day, they handed us a gift certificate to a bed and breakfast, some cash, and a note saying that Nicki would keep Ben whenever we chose to get away. (They offered to take the other kids too.)

We will never forget that beautiful gift of love and understanding. In those first ten years of Ben's life, we didn't get much sleep—five hours a night max. Many parents of developmentally disabled children are going through these endless nights right now, and my heart goes out to you. The gift was a reminder, at a crucial time, that we weren't alone. I hope it is a reminder to my readers to encourage someone in your circle of friends and acquaintances in whatever way you can, today!

My parents and Ed's parents wear giant halos today. Being loving, indispensable grandparents to Ben counts! Ed's mom often slipped me little devotionals or poems she had kept over the years, reminding her of those with special needs and special callings. All four grandparents spent many hours babysitting our children, including Ben, and they treated him like any of the others.

Ed's mom had a license plate that began "MLB." She always referred to it as her reminder of "my little boy"—her special endearment for the grandson who carried their name. Their love and support were invaluable to Ed and I. They provided overnight care when, really, they were too old to take on that kind of commitment. They never complained. They made each of our children feel special. It was not a word reserved for Ben. Their love was tangibly felt, and they are forever missed.

There were people at church who took it upon themselves to help with Ben all by themselves, without any program—like Bill and Shelley. They would entertain Ben in the hope that Ed and I could attend a whole worship service or go to Sunday School without getting a call from a distressed teacher. Bless them! Our friend Debbie is another. She now has a grandson with special needs as well, and is the special needs coordinator for the large church where Ben left his mark.

Some tried to include Ben in their Sunday school classrooms. They struggled, often calling us out of class in desperation. All of them get a massive round of applause for trying!

Ben's sisters are some of those beautiful saints. The two oldest usually ended up with Ben in their class, bearing the brunt of the stares and disgust of the other children who could not understand the odd behaviors and crazy sounds that came from Ben. Few, including adults, realized that Ben might have looked like an average, even handsome boy, but his "terrible twos" extended many years past that chronological age. Ben is in his thirties now, and when he is without proper medication—sometimes even with it—we still see that two-year-old combatant.

I'm hoping this book will be an encouragement to all those saints who played such a vital role in helping us raise Ben, at whatever stage we were at. Many were there for a season. Others were there longer. We moved about sixty miles north when Ben was fourteen, so we lost touch with many of those saints over the years.

I have decided that halo guy out front and to the right is Doug the Candy Man! He once sent Ben a whole bag of candy when he missed him at our new church. In Ben's drawing, the hat on the smiling face to the right looks a little like a chef's hat. That is fitting also, since Doug was chief chef at all breakfasts and dinners at that church.

I think the big smiley figure who looks like he's wearing a long tie, front and center, might be Kent. He is a fun-loving Swedish pastor with a booming voice. He had the distinctive honor of baptizing Ben in our pool. To make it comfortable for Ben, a few of our family members joined him. Kent has an enormous laugh and a heart to match. When we started a training program at our new church to recruit helpers and respite givers, Kent and his wife Sue were among the first volunteers. Have I told you yet about Ben's drooling? Kent and Sue took Ben to a movie with their family of boys and had a great time, but quickly learned *not* to share a straw with Ben—especially when he's engrossed in a movie!

We visited with Kent recently. He asked about Ben and started giggling, remembering a scene that happened years ago. Ben's favorite sport was to point his finger at someone and pretend to shoot them. Every day! Kent was watching one Sunday morning, he said, when Ben pointed that playful finger at a stodgy, often grumbling older parishioner. To Kent's amazement, the gentleman clasped his chest and fell to the floor with much theatrical flair, pretending to be dead. Immediately Ben paled and ran the other way. Kent saw both of the players through new eyes.

Kent's wife Sue gave us a different kind of support. She had three sons and no daughter, so she sewed darling clothes for almost all the little girls in our church. Among the favorites were outfits matching those worn by the American Girl doll that was so popular then. She took the time to bring attention and lavish gifts on Ben's siblings. She listened as our youngest two, Aubrey and James, read books for her so she could personally praise them on their academic progress. That was a gift I cherish to this day.

Another saint we met following our move was Ken. He was usually without a tie. He and his wife Shirley helped many young people over the years, and he always had a soft spot for our Ben—so much so that Ken dared a solo fishing excursion with Ben. For years afterward, Ben signed "fishing" whenever he saw Ken.

Another Ken was a husband to Ben's favorite aide at school, Thelma. They invited Ben into their home on several weekends to give us respite during those particularly tricky years between fourteen and eighteen years of age. They were gracious and loving hosts to Ben, who rarely returned the favor with grace. Thelma still has a special place in Ben's heart and is a friend of mine. I didn't know until years later that she has a sister who requires special care as well. I love that couple!

Others tried to help, but Ben wouldn't comply. Many wanted to help but were too scared. One great family decided to invite Ben along to a sporting event. They said they had a great time, but confided that they hadn't realized Ben needed help with his toileting needs. They described how Ben—standing nearly six feet tall at that time—came out of a bathroom stall and eagerly greeted a stranger with his booming "Hahee!" followed by a warm embrace and characteristic kiss. That scenario made the family too nervous to try again.

They most likely look back at that night as a funny, stretching experience. I know they're some of the happy faces in the crowd of saints who have come into Ben's life, then faded away. Whether happy or scared, loving or fearful, Ben *never* forgets a face. *Never*. People usually don't forget him either!

One of Ben's greatest friends is Dave Klaver—a friend who took the challenge to pray for Ben's healing to great lengths and prayed, consistently—every Tuesday—first, for Ben's healing, then in later years he would ask for updates on "how" to pray for Ben. He sent Ben Birthday and Christmas cards—often with presents, even when the possibility of meeting with Ben became too difficult—both for Ben and for him. What a gift he has been to us, and a faithful witness to our family.

I was privileged to sit in on Dean Nelson's writing class at the Calvin College Festival of Faith and Writing a few years ago. Dr. Nelson (http://deannelson.net) is the coauthor of *The Power of Serving Others*. In it, he and Gary Morsch describe the little and great acts of service that transform others' lives. In the workshop, he shared the example of a "little, bent-over neighbor lady" who came to his home to provide relief for his son, who was in a half-body cast at the time. He described the memory of his son lying on the living room floor, "guffawing" as this elderly neighbor batted a balloon to him from a chair across the room.

When Dr. Nelson gave us that word picture, it brought me right back to our first, tiny house and the many volunteers who came for patterning therapy for Ben. I'm thinking specifically of the little children who came along, providing the necessary diversion for Ben. They timidly approached him and repeatedly fell "dead" when he played his favorite game, causing him to laugh so hard he would lose his breath with every theatrical fall.

"Inclusion" isn't a regular part of some saints' vocabulary, and certainly wasn't in the mid-eighties, when we were struggling. *Exclusion*, I'm afraid, is still a genuine part of Ben's world. It wouldn't be fair to the whole story, nor would it do justice to the truth to gloss over the hard rejections we encountered as Ben grew. There was a time when the saints didn't look quite so beautiful. It's essential to note it here because it slowly became the norm for Ben.

Ed was working one Wednesday night, so Ben had to come with me to an awards night at church for our girls. It was an annual celebration, when children received their awards for memorization and projects completed. There was no longer a place for Ben in his sisters' classes, and no one with the foresight to make it work, so I had avoided church on Wednesdays. He didn't seem to mind—until that night.

The music started, announcing the parade of boys and girls. They marched in, wearing new scarves, singing songs, and waving to their parents. Ben jumped up, fighting my arms to go join them. He begged to march with his peers. I physically held him down. No one appeared to see his pleas or my torrent of tears as we watched the other boys receive badges. No one saw Ben signing, "Me! Please!"

I wished I had enrolled him and gone with him each week. Realistically, though, I didn't have the energy or the will to fight for him. I didn't want to draw more attention to him—or his sisters—either. I probably could have taken him to the friendship club—a unique ministry at another church in town—but I wasn't ready to explain his needs to yet another group of people, help him navigate yet another environment.

There were no badges prepared for this young boy who would never memorize verses or recite the books of the Bible. Yet he *knew*. He recognized each face and knew he was supposed to be in that lineup. He would never be able to understand why I held him back, nor why they forgot him.

Take a glance at Ben's drawing again, the complete one at the beginning of this story. Remember the two rows of little humps? I suggested those humps represent the people in the back row of Ben's life.

I looked at that picture for a few years before I realized there's a Ben signature in it too. Do you see it? Characteristically, "B" is sitting in the back also—with the spectators. But look! There's someone nuzzled up against him, and that person has *eyes*!

Could that smiley face be you? Are you reminded of a person even now whom you've felt drawn to and wondered how you could help, or if help was even possible? I encourage you to leave the spectator seat and take one small step closer to someone. It takes time, and it takes eyes!

CHAPTER 18

Baby Jacob

The privilege of the journey

If he was born alive, doctors said, he would have hours or minutes to live outside of his mother's womb. If he lived at all. His mother and father chose to carry this baby to full term, so he would live the majority of his earthly life in the safety and comfort of his mother's womb.

But Baby Jacob was no ordinary miracle. On the appointed day, almost fully developed, he lived through that crucial first gasp of breath, then through the early hours with hospital staff, friends, and strangers peeking into the room, amazed at his survival. He enjoyed his mother without any visible stress.

Into the next day, he continued to breathe. Family and friends took pictures of his tiny hands and feet, his pixie face beneath the soft, clean, knitted bonnet. Tearfully, sacredly, they took turns holding him and accepting the warmth and love of him. I was overjoyed by his parents' invitation to cuddle him, kissing his little pink face and offering a whispered prayer.

With nurses and doctors marveling, and thousands of prayers offered, he lived into the second day. On the third day, his parents met with hospice services and then carried Baby Jacob to the comfort of their home.

He was surrounded by his siblings, aunts, uncles, cousins, and grandparents. The home shone with life and energy. With hearts wide open to the impending parting, the family packed a lifetime of living and loving into each hour.

A week after his birth, I visited, again feeling the burden of their sorrow mixed with their joy in this precious life. I held him then too—a beautiful, wide-eyed babe, smelling of baby lotion and tender care. He always wore a soft cap, a pastel, protective reminder that a section of his skull was missing.

Baby Jacob was born to Ben's cousin Tammy and her husband Brian on March 11, 2004.

We all knew he would not live long, but he outlived all the educated guesses, dying in their arms twenty-one days later—on Ben's twenty-first birthday.

This drawing is an almost sacred depiction for me of that divine connection between Ben and his second cousin, though it was impossible for them to meet on earth. The little character even has a halo-like form on his head that reminds me of the little cap Baby Jacob wore.

There were no real similarities between Ben and Jacob. Unlike us, Brian and Tammy would only enjoy their precious son for a few short days. As Jacob's handsome young father entered the sanctuary, carrying the small casket to the front of the church, our hearts broke again. After nine months and only twenty-one days, Jacob's parents would close that chapter with their faith intact. Christians from around the world were praying for them and grieving with them, and now honored their brave and dignified choice for life.

I felt great sorrow for them over that abbreviated life, but feelings are never dependable and can be misunderstood—even by one's self. Again, I have to be painfully honest and acknowledge that

I was somewhat jealous of all the attention they were getting. I even felt envious that they would never know the agony we continued to experience because of Ben's years on earth.

At this point, Ben was still living in his first AFC house. I had registered legal complaints to the state regarding Ben's care. It didn't matter though; nothing ever changed. Nor could he come back home. Our experience and Ben's continued to be a hellish nightmare. (We learned, several years after Ben moved into the AFC home of our dreams, that that first home was, at last, closed.)

As Ed and I processed our emotions during the three weeks leading up to Ben's twenty-first birthday and Jacob's impending death, we talked about something many parents of special needs children know: we had buried many dreams during those twenty-one years. There had been no funerals. Most struggles we kept to ourselves. Flowers, words of love, and condolences were not part of our darkest nights and years. We did receive cards and notes from intuitive friends and family, but there was profound loneliness in Ben's sufferings, and it was challenging to actually grieve without feeling disloyal to Ben.

Jenny, Ben's oldest sister, wrote the blog I mentioned before, for several years—for people who loved "Benjamites." She wrote the following post in 2010, shortly before she met the wonderful man who would become our son-in-law and the father of our two grandchildren. It was titled, "Little Eulogies."[8]

The siblings of "Benjamins" know a totally unique kind of love and a devastating kind of suffering, and I think this excerpt beautifully depicts why.

> Beyond the obvious reason that everyone eventually dies, including Benjamites, I think the main reason [I write about this] is that loving a Benjamite involves so many tiny little deaths from beginning to end. Loss, loss, loss. Tiny little deaths in the secret places, the hopes and dreams keepers, the deep heart-spaces. Not "tiny" in the scope of their consequence, but small enough to fit into those deep places and not throw the world off course. A little death eulogized by a gulp and a blinked-away tear and nothing skips a beat. Like a little girl's summertime-playground recognition that her brother is taunted and teased, but she keeps swinging, pushing higher into the sky and wishing he would be normal. Loving a Benjamite means carrying a thousand little coffins and never knowing when a new one will open up and lay a piece of your heart to rest. Of course, there's nothing restful about it. No one imagines motherhood as a distant gaze from their toddler's gorgeous eyes and the emotionally draining attempts to connect with them all day. Little girls don't grow up thinking that their big brother won't have a conversation with them, ever. Grandparents don't expect to counsel and console sons and daughters who are

---

[8] Jen Boerema, "Little Eulogies" April 1, 2010, Little Tribe of Benjamin, https://littletribeofbenjamin.wordpress.com/?s=little+eulogies

exhausted, angry and heartbroken. Dads don't expect to try teaching their sons to shave while knowing that it will always be someone else's job.

The deaths on my mind in this season revolve around what happens if I get married and have kids, and how we'll include Ben in those things. A wedding won't be a good environment for him because of all the stress and excitement, and although I've always dreamed of him standing with the groomsmen, I don't think it would be a loving thing to make him do that for me. And when I have kids, there'll be other deaths: the uncle he would have been if he were normal, the cousins he would have given my children, the hard decisions of when to let him hold my babies in his too-strong arms. It's hard to imagine a good compromise in those situations.

I think, though, that this is another one of his best gifts to me. It hurts a lot, yes. As a result, I'm not satisfied with simple answers to hard questions, and I don't think there's anything wrong with paradox. I don't expect life to be easy. Growing up with all those deaths made me a softer person, more in tune with the suffering around us and eager to look for grace, hope, and beauty."

Such a torrent of unexpected, unwanted emotions erupted at the birth of beautiful Baby Jacob. Ed and I had suffered four miscarriages many years before. Memories of those little lives rose to the surface again, waiting to be acknowledged, as we grieved Jacob with my seven siblings and their spouses, children, and grandchildren, listening to passages of comfort read and songs offered in worship.

I felt like I was a little crazy. Did I want Ben dead so I could have a funeral? No! Did I grieve? Yes! As Jen later described so well in this blog post, we lamented the typical life we could have enjoyed with Ben. I suffered too through those days of Jacob's life, sometimes screaming out to God (as if he didn't know) the list of all the things that made Ben's life so excruciatingly painful. I reminded him how much Ben had suffered. Scenes from recent heartbreaking years were seared into our memory. So many times Ben fought us or wailed out his grief as we tore ourselves away, leaving him standing in the street with one of his aides, arms stretched out, begging for us to take him home. His separation anxiety disorder made each parting permanent in his mind.

The things our other children had suffered and longed for with Ben were now added to the heap of pain we could barely endure. Everything about his adulthood was strange. And yes, in many ways, that made *us*—our family—strange. Odd. Different. Sorrow came bubbling to the surface like a volcano with no outlet. The unbearable had become standard. Our emotions were raw.

As comforting hymns and praise songs filled the sanctuary, I thought back a few days, to Ben's twenty-first birthday, the day Jacob died. My mind refused to stay in the sanctuary, on the darling pictures of Jacob on the screen. Near us sat my once-active brother, with his wife and children. A successful businessman and precious brother, just fifty-five years old. Bob was battling pancreatic cancer—as our father had, ten years earlier. We were all praying and hoping for healing, and Bob was doing everything in his power.

At some point that day, I made a conscious decision to employ that faith-filled service in a slightly different way than intended. Tammy and Brian had probably prayed that others would be touched that day through whatever means God wanted to speak to friends and relatives coming. For me, it became a ceremony for all the things I would never experience with our four little ones lost to miscarriage, and the life we would never know with Ben. Between deep sighs, I sang out my faith, knowing that God was in control of it all.

> "Loving a Benjamite means carrying a thousand little coffins and never knowing
> when a new one will open up and lay a piece of your heart to rest."[9]

Ed and I leaned into one another, and our children, singing songs of worship and praise in that sacred place, singing to the God who knows about heartache. "It is well with my soul,"[10] we breathed out, sharing in the deep sorrow and steady faith of Jacob's family while reaffirming our faith in God. He is the One who, indeed, does all things well, whether it be in little lives that are never born alive; a darling one just twenty-one days old; our young man, twenty-one years old; or the precious brother hoping and praying for a fifty-sixth year that will never come on earth. That day, in that holy place, we gave God the glory for all those lives so divinely intertwined by and for Him.

Over the years I wondered about and was somewhat embarrassed by my attitude during that time. I asked God why I had been so grief-stricken for myself and for our family, when my niece and her husband had borne such a tragic loss and done so in such a beautiful way, sacrificing their precious time with Jacob to the rest of us in many ways.

Like it or not, emotions are as impossible to harness and control as the bipolar, manic episodes that rise in Ben, coming in like tidal waves, leaving no room for discussion or analysis. Grief *is*! "Little Eulogies" *must* be given.

It was six years later—March 18 to be exact. I'd been thinking about Jacob, Tammy, Brian, and Jacob's siblings a lot. That night I woke from a very vivid dream. Immediately rising, I messaged my niece this private note:

March 18 at 1:54 a.m.

---

[9] Jen Boerema, "Little Eulogies" April 1, 2010, Little Tribe of Benjamin, https://littletribeofbenjamin.wordpress.com/?s=little+eulogies
[10] "It is Well with My Soul", Horatio G. Stafford, "Timeless Truths Free Online Library", https://library.timelesstruths.org/music/It_Is_Well_with_My_Soul/

Dear Tammy, I had a very clear dream just now, and woke realizing it was about you and Jacob, so I'm writing it for you and what I think it meant. You actually were lying on my lap for some reason, and I realized you were thinking about Jacob. The pain was so clear, and I brushed your hair with my hand to help ease the pain, and help you sleep. There were others there too, but it was your lovely face that I saw. Then, as I awoke, I saw Jacob's beautiful little pixy face, and I was so glad to see him!

I started to count off on my fingers, from March 11 and realized it was exactly a week that you would have been holding him these six years ago. A beautiful, painful, so bitterly sweet week. You have a very special place in my heart as we share the gift of these special, special sons.

I'm praying for you again, for the peace that comes from loving that beautiful child tonight.

You're a special Mom. Please accept a cyber hug from your aunt Shar, dear one, and give one to your precious hubby too. I'm glad Jacob's life strengthened your love, as Ben has strengthened ours, through sorrow, and through the privilege of the journey.

Her response: March 19 at 8:47 p.m.

So precious. I have goose bumps! Thanks so much for sharing this. I remember you came with one-week birthday balloons for Jacob on that day as well! We definitely have a special heart connection. I think it is one of the blessings that God gives when we walk through those hard times. You know, you can tell almost immediately when talking with someone if they have been through an experience of seasoning. They are the kind of people you want to sit down and talk more with and learn from what they have learned. I wouldn't trade the experience for anything in the world.

The wonder of having held Jacob in our arms and having kissed his face, as Tammy said, left us with an enormous gift. I'm so grateful to have experienced these lives, all gifts. Thank you, Lord, for our babies in heaven. Thank you, God, for Jacob. Thank you for my brother, Bob.

And thank you so much for our Ben.

CHAPTER 19

Twenty-First Birthday and a Limo Ride

Difficult times don't outweigh the great ones

A journal entry from March 30, 2004:
Here in the night, it calls—Ben's book. I should be sleeping, but it
doesn't quit. I should be working on the things Jenny needs. Soon
she's leaving to spend a year of her life overseas, but still it beckons
me. I'll just tell about life as it is and as it was with Ben, and intersperse
it with Ben's artwork—his silly, insane, childish drawings. Tomorrow—no,
today is his twenty-first birthday! The chauffeur has his instructions. This is a
birthday I want to celebrate for two special hours … 120 minutes of pampering
us, not just Ben! There'll be flowers for Jen, Rachel, Aubrey, and me. There will
be balloons for Ed and James, and maybe grandparents too? Tomorrow.

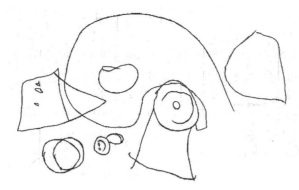

Ben drew this picture during the month of his twenty-first birthday. A whale? The limo? Balloons? Maybe all!

Ben's dad is a lover of vehicles: old cars, muscle cars, trucks, motorcycles, current sports cars—any kind. He often picks up the latest *Auto Trader* (a car buyer's catalog) and enjoys daydreaming. That publication is usually the first thing Ben finds when he comes home to visit. The big white limousines often caught his attention. He would point to himself, then punch the picture. "Muhmuh!" he screeched, making sure I knew what he was thinking.

"You'd like a ride in a big shiny limo, Ben? Would you take us for a ride with you?"

"Yah," he slowly exhaled, eyes already on the next page, catching himself drooling a little over a red truck (his perennial favorite).

With his twenty-first birthday looming, we struggled to think of what to get Ben that would give the day significance and be something he would say he liked if he could speak. That image of his request came back repeatedly. Hadn't he been asking for something he wanted for quite some time?

I planned for months to make that day special, including reserving a limo and having "21" embroidered onto a hat. We got that for his birthday so he could tell others about his big surprise. (The hat disappeared quite mysteriously within a week!)

I baked and took cupcakes to school that day. Ben greeted me with wild eyes, confirming his extreme edginess. His wonderful teacher Linda and the aides—including Bob, who had been with Ben since he first went to that school at fourteen years of age—crossed their fingers at me (behind Ben's turned back) and gathered all his classmates in the room across the hall.

Elizabeth sat at the edge of the table, her silent, sightless world suddenly brightened as her hands hit on the sweet gift of celebration. Josh stood as tall as me in the newly purchased device that lifted him out of his wheelchair and braced him into a standing position for the first time in his life. He looked so proud, still not looking directly at me, but flailing his forearms as usual, waiting for his treat. Danny would have eaten five cupcakes, so the teachers stopped him from reaching for more.

Ben waited with hands clasped to his chin as I slipped a candle into his cupcake. "Ah," he gasped as his candle burned for a few seconds, then was quickly extinguished by his excited blow. *Does Ben make wishes?* I asked silently. *Does he know how to wish? How to dream? Does he hope?*

Yes. I knew he expected things he wanted, like going home with me or hoping to get a pop. He would slap his left fist with his right palm and point to himself. "Yah?"

"Yes, Ben, we'll stop for a pop on the way home," I would promise.

Typically, Ben rode from school to his AFC home in the van belonging to the corporation that managed his house—the dreaded house he'd been at for almost three years. Today, I was taking him to our home to await his surprise.

After each child ate his or her treat, and we had opened little presents for all, I reached for the flower box hidden under the table and offered Ben's teacher and aides a tribute of our love and thanks.

Next, Ben and I traveled down the hall to Sheila's room. Sheila was the head of the crisis intervention team. These last months, as we dealt with Ben's explosive, aggressive, increasing bouts of bipolar mania, she had been busy. Ben needed to hand a flower to her personally!

Then we knocked at Thelma's door. Ah, Thelma! Short, petite, she had been an aide in Ben's classroom ever since he moved to that school—almost seven years. Her gifts were many, but her personality was orderliness; clean counters, chairs, dishes. She was continually tidying up after endless messes. She and her husband, Ken, had offered their time and home as a respite to us over the years. Willingly, they had sacrificed several peaceful weekends to give us rest. Ben loved her. So did I!

He eagerly handed her the remaining flowers. She asked me what she could get for his birthday. Laughing, I responded that a drive to Burger King would probably be the ultimate gift. Ben smiled and squealed his delight; she blushed in his warm embrace. Gripping his hands together, he jumped up and down. "Yup, Thelma, I think Burger King will be a great gift!"

She grinned shyly. "He's my Ben." She leaned in and reminded me softly, tenderly, "He'll always be my Ben."

One of the occupational therapists gave me a warm hug and some philosophical thoughts on our way out: "It never ends for these parents. No funeral. No resolution. Broken dreams." Putting empathetic words to Ben's endless difficulties, she gave me the gift of shared pain that particular day. She is a family friend and knew I didn't always see the negatives; she also recognized that the difficult times didn't outweigh the great ones. I didn't need to apologize for my tears.

Brand-new, tiny green leaves were just appearing on the sugar maples lining our farmyard. We were playing ball outside when we spotted the shiny white limousine approaching, about a quarter mile away. "Look, Ben! Look what's coming down the road!" As it pulled into the driveway, Ben characteristically got very shy, running toward the spring beauties popping up by an outdoor bench.

Smartly dressed, a dapper gentleman stepped out of the car and tipped his hat to us. Next, he pulled a long red carpet from the trunk and laid it in front of the passenger door, rolling it all the way onto the grass. He motioned for Ben to come. We helped Ben get his bearings. Then we all piled into the limo's showy, red-leather luxury—Ben in the middle.

Our chauffeur complimented us on our beautiful farm, circled the drive, and headed to the highway. Ben opened presents. We poured bubbling juice into plastic champagne glasses, turned on some rock and roll music, and felt pretty spoiled that bright spring evening.

Thirty rollicking minutes later, we picked up Jen from the busy accountant's office where she worked. It was two weeks before the April 15 tax deadline and just one month before she would leave for a year-long mission in Croatia. Graciously, she tucked away her lists and her nerves and walked ceremoniously down the red carpet into Ben's explosive exclamations and kisses.

Next stop: Ben's favorite restaurant, to order his favorite meal—McDonald's to go! I still giggle when I think about the grand white limousine pulling up to the service window. Then on we partied to Holland, an expensive decision that added at least an hour to the bill.

Our kind driver pulled up in front of a condo building and ushered Grandma and Grandpa down the same red carpet into the family's clapping joy. After the whole crew was driven around the block, we dropped Grandma and Grandpa off with hugs, returned her to the fray, then headed north.

When we were back in our car (which we had left parked near Ben's AFC home) we headed to his house. Ben grew tenser by the minute. He screamed, thrashed, and begged to stay as we pulled him from the car. Again, we had to leave him in the street with one of his aides, crying after us.

Those screams and desperate cries hovered over Ed and I as we sat together at Baby Jacob's funeral a few days later—that one, along with many other losses over twenty-one years.

But, looking back through the rearview mirror, we're happy we took the time to give Ben's "legal" birthday a toast. We are glad for the memory. The birth and life of this amazing young man deserved a limo ride.

CHAPTER 20

Only For Grown-Ups

Grow up!

I have a tender and loving view of Ben that lingers, painting right over the hard years and challenging places. If you've ever spent time with Ben or the Benjamins in this world, you probably feel the same.

I had five stressful calls on this day, though, regarding Ben's med review, behavior problems, aggression, and so on. The phone rang yet again, and I groaned at the caller ID. A friend, yes—but one with marriage problems. The marriage was the second one for both partners—I'll call them Nancy and Duane—and it was frayed and weak. They were good friends of ours, and over the years, Ed and I had invested in them, loved them, encouraged them and worked with them through several near-divorce moments.

If you look at the picture Ben drew here, he was *not* having a good day. Everything was scratched out and scribbled through with heavy markers and no happy, peaceful lines. But, in the top right corner, notice the smiley face. It didn't fit, but he got it in there on a bad day!

I could hear depression in Nancy's voice. She rehearsed her despair over his latest spiteful words and groaned that she was too tired to deal with marriage problems. It wasn't worth it anymore. "I just want out!"

"You know, I totally understand," I wearily agreed then. "Ben's problems are overwhelming. I want out sometimes too."

We had hidden Ben's many physically aggressive outbursts in the past to protect his reputation. That day, I didn't have the energy to hide my agitated mental state. I shared more than ever, blurting out the worst of his behaviors and our fears, and how it felt to have him take all the attention that our other children deserved and needed.

Concerned, she asked me, "Isn't it going well for Ben?"

I realized then how clueless people were. Most assumed we had placed Ben in adult foster care and that was that, that somehow his life went on like other grown children. She didn't know his daily struggles were anything but ordinary.

I explained that it had been over three years since Ben's significant behavioral changes and aggression sent us looking for a foster home. For many months now, I had been getting almost daily calls or emails regarding Ben's violent behavior *again* at school. I was depressed but reminded her (and myself) that God knew.

Nancy realized she didn't understand anything about our daily struggles. She wondered out loud how we could keep going with a ten- and an eleven-year-old at home, and young adult daughters leaving the nest, and why wasn't I crazy? I was grateful for a listening ear, and ended up sharing more than I ever had.

Later that day, something I'd heard years before came back to me. Mrs. Jean Lush was a social worker, lecturer, and author. She "had a delightful Australian dash of humor, often calling people 'Ducky'! She personified the spirit of her native Australia with a witty dash of derring-do," wrote the *Seattle Times*[11] when she passed away in 1996. The whole article is worth the read! Such an interesting woman!

In her smiling, lecturing voice, Mrs. Lush had charmed the interviewer and me, for sure, the several times I had enjoyed listening to her in the 1980s. Her words left a lasting impression on the young mother I was when she offhandedly commented—I'm using my own memory for this: *Americans love to tell their children to grow up.* Slightly sarcastic then, I remember her quipping that *parents* were the ones who needed to *grow up.* She explained that children need parents who aren't lazy but will do the hard work—parents who won't grow weary over the long haul. I have often replayed that thought when I've needed to *grow up* and *grow into* my role as a mother to Ben.

I recalled my lengthy complaint session on the phone earlier that day. I realized my "I can't" had been loud and clear. "I can do all things through Christ which strengtheneth me!" Phiippians 4:13 (KJV) had been stripped from my vocabulary!

Sometime during the next week, Nancy and I talked again. She asked how I was doing this time. I told her how I shared that to give thanks "in all things" meant—for me—this ongoing situation with Ben. We both had seen that verse many times, in different conditions, whether job-related, financial, or parental. I said that God had somehow given me a fresh reminder of his love and care for anything and everything that concerns me.

My surroundings were the same: I was sitting on the same couch, holding the same telephone, looking out the same window as the week before—and Ben's behaviors had continued. But this time I felt almost giddy while Nancy and I talked.

I explained my puzzlement: formal letters of complaint to the state; searching for another house for Ben; more meds; different meds; meetings with psychologists, teachers, and caseworkers. *Nothing* had changed in Ben's situation. But turning it over to God again that week, deciding to *thank* God for these circumstances and this trial, had bubbled up hand-clapping, singing joy for me!

What Nancy said surprised me. When we had last spoken, she quietly said, my honesty had spoken to her heart, reminding her of the tremendous blessing she had in her husband of ten years. She began to thank God for Duane, even if he never changed, and she began to give praise for her marriage.

I believe that was the last time I ever got a desperate call from her. Their problems haven't all gone away, of course. Some things in their lives have gotten more difficult. But, praise God, they have been married for over twenty years at this point.

Life isn't easy for anyone. *We all have challenges.* Some days have enormous pains, some have small irritations, but God promises peace and joy in every circumstance if we will literally turn it over to him.

It was some months later that God finally opened a new home for Ben. It solved many of his

---

[11] Carole Beers, Reporter, "Jean Lush, 82, Social Worker Who Did Everything `With Flair'", June 9, 1996, The Seattle Times, http://community.seattletimes.nwsource.com/archive/?date=19960609&slug=2333575

problems and gave him greater dignity, more freedom, and better care than I could have dreamed we would find. We have enjoyed that relationship now for almost fifteen years. The bipolar episodes and severe separation anxiety still disrupt Ben's life and ours. But, praise God, we have seen a marked improvement in Ben's life circumstances over the years. When we handed the situation over to God, we watched as God removed obstacles and even challenging people from Ben's life. Most important to us, Ben is surrounded by people who care deeply for him.

Quitting, walking away, giving up? Sometimes it's necessary. But, with God's grace, there are new lessons and new blessings to be learned. Marriage, like parenting, is *only for grown-ups*!

CHAPTER 21

A Brother's Giant-Size Touchdown

For your brother Jim and his brother, Ben! I mean it! Go Wildcats!

For my husband, Ed, missing football practices was one of the hardest things about living in Minneapolis. Other than Special Olympics, which was a lot of fun, Ed waited years to watch a son compete. For four years he hung out at most practices, often leading the team in prayer before games. But he felt disconnected this season.

Ed never had to travel for business before, but Michigan's economy had imploded. In 2006, he was offered the opportunity to model the 2010 Polaris motorcycle and build a realistic prototype of it. It was a chance to make some money again, to use his skills as a design sculptor with one of his best friends, Ray, and to spend some time around motorcycles. It was all good—except this opportunity was 650 miles from home!

I packed up James and Aubrey often to meet Ed in Minneapolis. We headed west for a week during their summer break. I like to drive, so many weekends saw us making the twenty-four-hour round-trip through Chicago and back. We did okay with the end of winter and welcomed spring, comparing birds and wildlife. Then the waiting got long.

"Giant Slayers All" was Ed's nickname for our family. We felt like we did pretty good at slaying the giants of attitude corrections, and of tiring weekends traveling, and for taking care of things on the farm without him there. Giants of loneliness, job demands, and communication problems toppled as we slung our weapons. But sickness, the life-threatening variety of giant, almost toppled our resolve.

Ben, then twenty-three, was taken to the emergency room after several days of congestion. They called me, and I met his supervisor Eric there. Ben was having a hard time breathing. Thinking this was my responsibility, I thanked Eric and sent him home. Ben was admitted and moved to a regular room on a regular floor of the hospital.

All through that night, hiss condition worsened and his fever rose. During the first few hours, he was treated by an intuitive doctor, a pulmonary specialist, who played "the breathing game" with him. But as the night wore on, Ben became steadily more agitated in that cold world of strangers and bright lights, and his breathing became much more labored.

I spent the night in his room, putting on pajamas that Rachel brought. She was involved in an internship and work, but she brought me supplies, then headed home to take my load there on her shoulders also. Ed and the others on his work team were putting the finishing touches on the motorcycle until two in the morning. He got frequent updates from home until communication ended early in the morning. Ben worsened every hour.

When a respiratory specialist was called in, somewhere around midnight, I didn't understand his broken English, nor what he meant by the term *ventilator*. I was too upset, too tired, too scared to think straight. We had previously decided we weren't going to use any "heroics" on Ben if it was his time to die, but I was confused about where a ventilator fit in that scheme of things. I said no, but I couldn't believe we'd come to that so quickly.

Desperately, I asked a nurse to explain the procedure and requested that she call the doctor back in. But the doctor never returned. I knew Ben had to have thickened drinks, but he was dehydrated. I consciously let him sip from a cup of ice chips when he kept signing for a drink. Chips weren't thickened, of course, but I was feeling helpless. Things would spiral from bad to much worse.

Ben is a very private person. I tried to keep the intravenous lines attached as he signed his persistent need for a bowel movement. Back and forth from bed to bathroom we trudged, in futile attempts at toileting. The hospital gown added to his embarrassment and misery. He refused nurses' help, and I knew he would fight if I pushed, since he felt threatened.

He is usually a little off balance when he walks, but at that point he was exhausted and very ill. He swiped and moaned at me to leave, while crazily tearing at the attached tubing. I told the nurses of his desperate need for an enema, but they didn't take action. I'm sure they couldn't without a doctor's order. They probably didn't want to administer one to a fighting man, and they apparently considered constipation the lesser of his problems.

Finally, Ben turned on everyone in sight, literally screaming out for help, wrestling for breath. That's when he got the help he needed, around seven in the morning. He was restrained by security, and finally moved to critical care. They quickly put him into an induced coma so that they could begin icing him down. His fever had topped 104 degrees.

This picture reminds me of the hat nurses used to wear, and of the wonderful nurses
and respiratory therapists who cared for Ben in the critical care unit.

When I saw the critical care staff's quick, quiet, controlled response to Ben's needs, it was apparent he should have been in that department all night. Within a few hours, he was intubated and on a ventilator. Eric came that morning and joined me at Ben's other side, massaging his arms, assuring him of our presence.

I knew then I would never again handle Ben's crises alone. All I had to do was call, and Eric or Ben's Community Health nurse would be there. I realized—too late—that Ben would have been better served if professionals had been with him throughout this event, instead of his emotional mom.

After seven grueling months of long days, Ed's team finished the motorcycle early that Friday morning. Following about three hours of sleep, he packed his bags, loaded the truck, and floored it—well over the speed limit. He powered through pouring rain for about six hours, checking his watch. All phone communication between us had ended as Ben's battle escalated. Ed didn't have any GPS then, so he frantically searched for signs that would lead him to the Badger—a ferry that crossed Lake Michigan, and the fastest route home, versus the lengthier drive through and around Chicago. As if that weren't enough pressure, it was the last day of the year that the Badger would run.

It was a very rough crossing. Someone had broken their arm while being tossed around on the Badger's prior trip. But Ed was too tired to mind. When it reached port in Ludington Michigan, after four hours, the vehicles were unloaded, and Ed drove another hour home.

Meanwhile, doctors gave me very little hope. We prayed. Friends and family from many churches gathered and prayed. The prognosis for this giant was grim and, without sleep, I was weak with fear. The doctors thought Ben's illness was probably caused by silent aspiration—the possibility of food or liquid being inhaled and causing pneumonia. They talked about the possible need for a permanent stomach tube, bypassing the esophagus and the aspiration problem.

I broke down completely at the mere mention of that looming giant. Eating had always been one of Ben's biggest pleasures in life.

At home, without complaining, Rachel somehow added my job to her own—making sure the kids got off to school, plus an internship in occupational therapy, crucial to her degree. Jen lived in an apartment and had recently started school again, hoping to complete a degree in journalism at Michigan State University.

They both came to be with Ben that Friday night. We noted how Ben's heart rate lowered and oxygen levels improved when we held his hand. Often he gripped our fingers in return—whether by reflex or intention, we didn't know. A narrow recliner became my bed as I held his hand and reassured his quiet body.

Ed got home at 9:45 that night, having slept about eight hours in the last sixty. After catching a few winks, he spent most of Saturday with us in critical care, trying to take it all in.

On Saturday night Ed and I left for a few hours' sleep while his sisters held Ben's hands. Friends stopped by with food and presents for Ben. He had great nurses and specialists, attentive to every need, asking us for his story.

While Jen and Rachel were singing to Ben that night, someone stole Jen's laptop, which held all of her life's connections. Because she had spent a year in Croatia, the laptop was the only consistent "home" she'd had for many months. All of her essential papers were gone.

We learned from surveillance video that we had seen and even talked with the man who watched us come and go all through the day and into the night, without any hospital authorities asking why he was in the critical care family waiting room. When he found the perfect opportunity, he stashed Jen's laptop under his jacket and walked right out of the hospital. Police never captured him or retrieved the computer.

We prayed together about this newest giant: "Father, give us wisdom. Help us to forgive. Bring good from this somehow."

Jen didn't feel she could continue school without a computer, and with Ben so seriously ill, she couldn't concentrate on anything, let alone try to rewrite all the papers she'd been working on. Ed and I agreed she should withdraw from classes for the time being.

Jen set up a blog site, *Giant Slayers*, from a public computer in the family lounge, letting people all over the world know how to pray for Ben, for our family, and now for her. She was never able to return to Michigan State, but God provided other opportunities for her to pursue, and she's grateful for the intangible things she learned during those hard times.

We watched and hoped through the days and nights as the most potent antibiotics made no difference. Ben's oxygen levels remained barely acceptable. A new medicine brought his temperature down, yet the rhythmical whooshing of the ventilator (a machine pumping oxygen directly into his lungs) was an endless, resonating reminder of his peril. We sat staring at numbers that would not budge.

With every hour, I was getting an education on what the diagnosis of silent aspiration meant and what it could cost. "I don't like what I see," the doctor confessed. "Aspiration pneumonia is always difficult." He showed us a new set of X-rays that looked worse than the day before and gave us no encouragement. "It's possible Ben may get worse before he gets better," he warned. Ben did.

We had many visitors throughout that week. Ben's teachers and aides came, and Evelyn prepared a lavish supper, encouraging us so much with her smile and her faith, not doubting for a moment that God was healing Ben. Ben had an army of people praying for him and hoping for our gentle giant's health.

Eight days after that first call from the emergency room, I stood shivering and tired on the cold tile floor, studying Ben's sedated body. Bruises crawled up and down both arms where IVs roamed and veins collapsed, or where they drew blood. His stomach was a pincushion of daily shots. Several times each day, they lessened the sedation to see Ben's responses. Quickly, he'd fight the strangers and swat at his tubes and needles. So they tied his arms to the bedrails to protect him from further injury. Saturday morning would be their next, hopefully successful try.

The regular nurses had become family by then and knew Ben and his diagnosis and behaviors pretty well. But that Friday night he had a new, eager nurse. I was in the recliner next to Ben, half asleep around midnight, drowsily wondering what she was doing. Apparently, she thought she was preparing him for an early morning attempt at breathing on his own, and she started taking him off the sedative. I warned her several times that we would need help if he regained consciousness, but she either didn't hear me or thought I was wrong.

Ben immediately realized he had IVs everywhere. His arms were restrained, tubes ran into his nose, and he gnashed his teeth on the large, plastic pacifier-shaped gadget holding the ventilation tube in place. Desperately he signed "drink" to me over and over as the nurse ran for help.

"No, honey. We can't," I replied. "Momma's so sorry! You're a brave boy, Ben."

It was an impossible situation for him. Trying to get out of bed, he lashed out at everyone, including me.

Of course, he failed the breathing test in the morning. His lungs were still too weak, and I felt just as frail, standing or sitting and praying by his bedside in that cold, sterile room while icy rain pelted the window. I wondered when and if this giant would fall.

That young nurse was inexperienced. She hadn't carefully read Ben's chart. When our favorite nurse, Julie, returned to work in the morning, she immediately made a thorough examination of Ben. She changed all his laundry and made sure everything was as it should be, not trusting anything about his treatment since her last shift. She told me then they only needed ten minutes for the sedation to begin to clear Ben's body—not hours, as the young nurse had claimed. Because of that mistake, it took several hours for Ben to get comfortable again. His stats took hours to return to the level we'd seen twelve hours before the situation started.

Around noon, I stared, maddened at those stats, protectively placing Ben's hand under the blanket. Amid angry tears, I walked to the window and stared out at the thick, gray clouds. All the frustrations of the past days bubbled up. Giant slayer? *Me?*

Morosely, I reviewed my coveted win of the *Guideposts* Writers Workshop Contest. The timing was ironic because I won it with a story about Ben! It had been a dream come true and came with a week's conference with the *Guidepost* editors in New York. Instead of celebrating that achievement, I had canceled the reservation as Ben's hospital stay lengthened. *Why would you give me something so encouraging, then take it away, God?*

I didn't stop there, letting my mind ruminate on the trauma in Jen's life, feeling ashamed she was a lot more positive about it than I was. *Jen was finally following her dream of going to school, and now that was gone! What are you doing, God?*

Meanwhile, Ed was enjoying being with the kids at home. I missed that too. I was sick of missing out!

The phone interrupted my melancholy thoughts. "Hello?"

"Honey, Ben will be just fine. He'll probably sleep all afternoon. Come and meet us at the game," Ed pleaded. "Please!"

I had only just left the hospital for short hours at a time these eight and a half days, and I reluctantly agreed—after confirming that Julie would be working.

Ed brought our son Jim (James) to the field that afternoon. Ed told me later that the coach approached him asking, "Tell me what's happening with Ben." Ed couldn't believe his next words: "I want you to know I'm going to ask the boys to dedicate this game to Ben. If it's all right with you, I'd like to pray with the boys."

A jostling amalgam of cleats, helmets, and padded-up eleven- and twelve-year-olds quieted themselves long enough to form a makeshift huddle, squinting while the coach prayed. "Today," Coach Collins said, "I want you to think of Jim as your brother. You know that Jim's brother is still in the hospital. He needs your help. Today I want you to go out there and take it home for your brother Jim and his brother, Ben. I mean it! Go Wildcats!"

They put their fists together in the huddle and roared their mightiest enemy-defying roar: "*Team!*"

Thankful the rain had stopped, my spirit soared at the sight of all those blue-and-white uniforms and the smell of fall in the air. I quickly found my three scarved daughters in the bleachers. I had just climbed to them, hugging each of them, when a roar went up. I caught sight of Jimmy charging behind the opposition's offensive line. With his mother and sisters screaming, "Go, James!" he sacked their quarterback! Right in front of us!

The announcer had barely barked out "Number 40, Jim Boerema with the sack!" when I stood, unbelieving, to watch him plow through the line of scrimmage, doing the same thing all over again!

"Gooooo, Jimmy!" I bellowed.

Before we got through that quarter, we all realized this had become a day of miracles, and Jimmy and Ben were first in line! Jimmy's size-twelve feet ran faster than ever, intercepting a pass and giving the ball back to our Wildcats. Later, when I asked him what he had been thinking, he said, "I just couldn't stop thinking about Ben, Mom."

Other parents turned around to congratulate us. I felt chills run up and down my spine as I caught my husband's eye, and he caught my hand. Something genuinely great was in the air. Within ten minutes, all of the morning's blues were washed away!

I made myself sit down again, joining my daughters, who were wrapped in blankets and munching popcorn. Our mittened hands held cocoa drinks that had turned as cold as the air.

Suddenly, from about the thirty-five-yard line, someone handed Jimmy the ball. He was sprinting, galloping, straining, running—all the way through the end zone!

Dick Smith, the announcer and a family friend, blurted, "That seals it for—" Then he stopped himself so he wouldn't demoralize the opponents, instead blaring out, "Touchdown, Number 40! A big day for Jim Boerema and the Wildcats!"

One of the moms called up, "What didja feed that boy for lunch?"

I had to ask his sisters, and giggling, yelled back, "Pizza, pretzels, and yogurt!" (I think I yelled a *lot* that afternoon.)

We all knew it wasn't the food. God was answering the prayers of hundreds, possibly thousands of people around the world and in that tight-knit community, all of whom were praying for Ben and for his family. It was *Life* cheering on a tired mom, wrapping his arms around sisters who loved their brothers more than their goals and dreams. *Hope* had heard the desperate cries of an exhausted husband and father.

Best of all, it was *Love* itself in the huddle, giving strength to those feisty boys, reminding a faithful coach that God *does* answer prayer. The giant, *Defeat*, was kicked right through the end zone as they raised their helmets, singing the Wildcat fight song when their victory was sealed.

Our normally quiet James couldn't talk fast enough later that afternoon. "My mouth guard kept falling out of my mouth 'cause I was smiling so big! It's the first time I remember praying when I made a touchdown!"

On Sunday morning, the giant, *Ventilator*, rolled right out of Ben's room. Ben did receive great care, but I believe the biggest turnaround came as eighteen boys gathered on that football field and one great coach said, "Today, Ben and Jim are your brothers!" Then they prayed. And the giants came tumbling down!

Oh, by the way, the brand of the Polaris motorcycle Ed was sculpting? Victory!

Ed, pictured here with *Victory's* designer, Mike Song.

CHAPTER 22

Sister Number Two and Graduation

Hoping to hear his first spontaneous word

The following letter, like the one written by Jen that I reproduced in chapter 10, describes the beauty, the sorrow, and the many gifts of grace that surround our family. Rachel, an Occupational Therapist, lives in California, working now as a Clinical Liaison at a rehabilitation hospital, in Santa Barbara. Her patients are often victims of stroke or trauma, or violence, sometimes newly paralyzed, or missing limbs, often coping with life-altering consequences.

Ben was graduating from the Wesley school he had attended from ages fourteen through twenty-six. Rachel hoped to make a trip home for the occasion, but she was spending late nights and weekends taking career classes online, with the goal of walking at her own long-anticipated college graduation.

Rachel had to miss Ben's graduation, but he had not been present for most milestones in her life, either. Often, we were unable to participate in significant events in Rachel's life because of our involvement with Ben's.

This letter was her loving tribute to Ben, including the deepest longings of her heart for her big brother.

From Jen's blog[12]

June 12, 2009

[Jen's introduction:] *This post is my sister Rachel's contribution to Ben's growing collection of written tributes. :) I love it so much. She captured how we felt growing up, and how we feel today, which is not an easy task! Love you, Rach!*

P.S. "Thumbs up" is a familiar phrase for anyone who works with Ben. When he's sliding into a bad attitude, sometimes all it takes to redirect him is a quick flip of your thumbs and the reminder—he'll smile a cheesy smile and if you're lucky you can move on to a different subject. Sometimes the attempt isn't quite so useful and ends up feeling like you high-fived a tornado and watched it plow through Main Street. :)

Tomorrow, my big brother will graduate from school. Not high school. Surely not college. Just school. He is twenty-six and mischievously cute, talented too—how many men can hit a one-inch pebble 25' with a child's plastic bat, while sitting in the light of the setting sun, huh? And do that over and over and over again while sitting on the ground with only the occasional break to push the dog out of the way. The guy's got talent.

This is a week that my family has anticipated for years, and each of us in our way. I think we

---

[12] Rachel Boerema, blog post "Milestones—Graduation, "Little Tribe of Benjamin" reposted May 29, 2010 *https://littletribeofbenjamin.wordpress.com/2010/05/*

grieve and share a joy for and with each other, but each one of us has bittersweet thoughts and tears that we own.

When I was growing up, Ben was the big brother I wanted—and I wanted him to know that. I talked to him—tried to tell him everything that was in my heart, tried to voice just how cool he was, fought with him, and bandaged his booboos. But, Ben could never really talk back. Some nights, I would hang out in his room and tell him about my day and try to talk him through the process of replying to what I was saying.

"Make this sound, Ben: Mmmm. Good! Now, Mmmm and ooooh together. No, almost! Mmmmm …" Other days, I would sneak glances in his direction, my ears attentive, hoping to hear his first spontaneous word other than "da" or "ma." I wanted to hear "Rachel." I wanted to hear, "This is what I did at school today—isn't that cool? Hey, let's go for a bike ride and then we can play football."

I remember one morning at home—I wasn't quite six when I thought Ben said "Good morning" as I walked by. I ran to my mom and excitedly told her what I was sure I'd heard. "Really? No, honey, I don't think so. I'm glad you are trying to hear him talk though."

Sometimes, trying to hear him talk, trying to imagine what his handwriting would look like, forming into legible letters and ultimately words and essays on his experiences as a handicapped child, stemming from a childhood hope that could not be extinguished. Really—why would little girl Rachel suspect Ben would be the same functionally when he was twenty as when he was 10? He went to school, right? He was Trainable Mentally Impaired, so he could be trained in the skills of being a normal guy, right?

Slowly, that beautifully naive hope altered—never left, but was changed by re-assessment that said, "Severely Mentally Impaired." Changed by my studies of the human brain. Maybe he wouldn't learn how to talk? Perhaps he wouldn't play hardcore tackle football with me? *What if he couldn't live on his own? Would I be able to take care of him when I grew up?*

For all that Ben could or could not do, I wanted to protect him … I hated it when my brother got the "Ben, be nice" treatment when he was just trying to figure out how to pet a puppy. Ben was strong and still is. While his strength frightened people, he was also tender and could spot a broken heart from 20 feet away. Ben felt the sting of those looks and words. Oh, how I hated to see him hurt.

Yesterday at work, a woman started weeping nearby and repeating in distraught and soul-wrenching tones, "No, no, no, no, no …" She has had few other words since her injury, and I had to leave the gym. I couldn't handle hearing what I had heard so clearly when I was little: when Ben came to the end of his rope to feel his inability to communicate or be understood, he would cry with words and sounds that only his tongue could form. And that was usually at home or while he fell asleep.

I miss being close enough to him to help calm him down when he is troubled. I feel like I have let him down as the protective sister. I moved away, and I couldn't even make it to his only graduation. His big day. His beautiful step into adulthood. I won't see his smile as he walks through his school gym to receive the recognition he earned. Benjamin Edward Boerema, Graduating Class of 2009.

Oh Ben, how many times have we talked about this big event for you? It's here now, and rumor has it you are ready. Ready to be accepted into the Wesley Roberts day program, prepared to move into the community beyond the warm and loving walls of Linda's classroom and Bob's watchful eye and jokes with you. You will do a great job with the transition, Ben, and you'll even be in the same program as your best bud Orion! In one week, my family will gather at my parent's farm for Ben's open house. I had planned to be home for it, but those plans fell through. I even looked at last-minute ticket prices again … I'm sorry, Ben. I know you will smile and giggle and hug all of your guests, basking in the spotlight on your life, but I am so sorry.

Ben, someday we might live side by side again. Last year, dad asked me if I had made a move that was temporary or for a career and life. I don't know, but I pray that I live near you again, dear heart. I pray that we will spend afternoons playing once again. That someday you will be the grandest uncle your sisters and brother could ever want for their children. That you will delight in the Fourth of July fireworks as if they were a new surprise that we planned each year just for you. That you will sing to me sweetly on the phone and hold my hand gently when we walk across busy streets.

Ben, I pray that you will have great joy as you close the chapter on school and open the door to new treasures of learning in life. I pray you find delight in the work of your hands, and that your heart remains tender to the love that you and Jesus share.

Thumbs up Ben, this is your green day!

Evelyn, on the left, was a beautiful Spirit-filled aide in Ben's room. Rachel mentions Linda, Ben's fabulous teacher—on the right, with Bob—friend, aide, and bowling coach to Ben!

CHAPTER 23

PCP Time

Taking each of my arms in his hands, placing them around his middle,
before holding me tightly and long

When we still lived on the farm and would drive Ben back to his new house after a visit, we had to take the same highway exit that led to the horrific first house where he had lived for four years on a street called, "Marcoux". Thankfully, we then turned east instead of west when driving to his new home. But if I mentioned "Marcoux," or pointed in that direction, he would always give a worried shake of the head, with his hands up: "stop." Before I finalized this book, I made a decision not to include another word about that place. Maybe another time, but not in this book.

In 2005, God answered the prayer of our hearts and opened the door to the Annette Street AFC Home, under the care and management of the MOKA Foundation. Ben's teachers and specialists had been telling me forever that we had to "get Ben in Eric's home." Of course, we couldn't force an opening, and during those four years, I never did meet this famous Eric. I just made the message loud and clear to Ben's caseworker that I wanted Ben in Eric's home.

We were desperate to get him out of the Marcoux Street house! In truth, we would have taken anything that looked better than the one he was in, but I kept knocking at Eric's door. That organization—MOKA—and particularly Eric and his staff, changed Ben's life. He had a marked decrease in behaviors almost immediately. His years there have given us hope that Ben's future might be a happy one.

This chapter is a description of Ben's yearly person-centered plan (PCP) meeting, typically held the month before his anniversary in the AFC home. [The PCP took the place of the special education IEP meeting for adults with special needs.] In this case, the meeting happened in July 2010 after five years in the MOKA home.

He was sitting on a chair in the corner of the dining room/kitchen when I arrived, waiting to surprise me. "Where's Ben?" I asked as I stepped in the door. "Oh, *there* you are!"

Noisily pushing the big, wooden chair back, he eagerly wrapped me in his signature hug: taking each of my arms in his hands, he placed them around his middle before holding me tightly and long. With the tips of fingers on both hands touching to form a peak, he waved his hands up and down and asked, "House?" several times.

"Nope, Mama's here for your big meeting!"

He was jumping at this point, barely moving his big body three centimeters off the ground.

"I'm staying right here. Then we're going to go to lunch together."

Grinning, he patted his palms together, turned them over, and slapped again: "hamburger."

I laid a fresh bag of bagels and cream cheese on the counter, then got an update from Ginger (one of the aides at his AFC home) as she cleaned. The dishwasher was chugging away. Quietly she confided, "We have our four-man house!" Immediately, she assured me no one had died, but that our friend with heavy-lensed glasses had moved out of the tiny 5-person house. Steve, the one with the firm handshake and unsteady gait. He had been the oldest member of the home, the generous maker and giver of beaded necklaces. Steve had now moved into a safer residence that had become available.

This was great news. Ben's friend got a safer home, and the rest of the men would finally each get a bedroom of his own. I commented that I would help clean out Ben's closet to prepare for the move.

The door alarm sounded as two women entered. Tucking one under his arm like a trophy, Ben eagerly kissed the top of Frances's head—a smiling, practically dressed, dark-skinned woman—while acknowledging Jill, the director of the day program Ben attended. The next arrival was his case manager, Sandy. Ben beamed like a kid out of school—which he was!

"Show us your new bedroom, Ben," I prodded. He grabbed my hand, half skipping his way down the narrow hall, leading the whole team to the last room on the left, now obviously brighter than on previous visits. With eyes sparkling, he turned his hand out, signing, "Here it is!"

"This is the office, Ben, not your room!"

"No," giggled the house manager, also beaming, like Ben, "This will be Ben's new room about a week from now. I had a door with windows put in to make a much brighter room and create the egress that was required."

"Wow, Ben. What a great room!"

But already Ben had moved back to another room, pulling my hand to follow. We stood in front of his current closet. "Ben! You're right! I did want to check out your closet this morning. You are on the ball!"

Time didn't mean anything to Ben, so he assumed this was probably the day. "Yah?" he squealed proudly. He still amazes me at times by the way he catches details in conversations he didn't seem to notice.

Thank you, God, for his joy and—and self-confidence in this tiny home, I silently prayed.

His manager gave me a tour of the approximately seventy-feet long by twenty-feet wide home, pointing out little and big changes they were making. Ben dropped off in the dining room, eagerly greeting more of his team as the door alarm sounded again. Eric pointed out that they'd replaced a chest freezer with a slightly rusty old upright, to make more room in the space he'd allotted himself—the "new" office at the back of the one-stall-garage-turned-living-room. "We're putting another door in here, with a window to let in more light. And we'll add a good door here, between the living room and office."

This house was nothing like the larger, newer home Ben had moved from. In fact, it was not up to par with an average home in West Michigan. But Eric did not complain. Though the staff worked for MOKA, Community Mental Health owned the structure. Eric and his staff had waited patiently for years for an upgrade, and this new living arrangement, though pinched, seemed to energize him for the work he loved.

"You gave up a great office, Eric," I said.

"No, the men finally each have a bedroom. This is going to be so much better!"

He returned to the kitchen to help Kathleen, who was grinding up Ben's bagel and cream cheese, softening it with applesauce. Ginger was fixing Ben's sugar-free flavored cream, with coffee added and thickened.

Ben's team! Slowly, comfortably, we took our places at the dining room table. The air conditioning was a welcome relief on this hot summer day. Ben, at the head, moved over when his case manager, Sandy, asked his permission to sit next to him. With her personal warmth and attention to details, she has proven to be very attentive and well-suited for the many demands of her job.

Kathleen—the psychologist who had weathered some of Ben's worst storms since meeting him nine years earlier, when he entered the adult foster care world—sat next to Eric. Ben's speech pathologist arrived just as we were getting settled, pulling up a chair between Kathleen and Eric. With fresh cups of coffee in hand and bagels all around, we were ready to begin.

I tore out a sheet of paper and pushed it toward Ben asking, "Which pen would you like, Ben?" Choosing the silver-and-purple one, he immediately began to draw. One of the pictures he drew depicted the scene before us pretty accurately. From the beginning to the end of his meeting, Ben was in charge. He teased Eric incessantly and made us all laugh out loud.

I think of the little circle at the top of this drawing as Ben seated at the head of the table. The scribbles could be an attempt at bagels and coffee mugs. I was sitting about where the other circle is falling off the edge.

Sandy called the meeting to order and asked Ben whom he would choose to start our session. "Mmmm," he said, putting his index finger to his lips. (*Drum roll, please!*) He thrust it toward Frances. She squirmed in her chair at the other end of the table, but smiled sweetly back at him. By the tremor in her voice and heightened perspiration on her brow, we knew meetings were not in her comfort zone, but she proceeded with her carefully written report.

Her eyes sparkled as she noted how Ben "especially loves the cooking class." We all agreed knowingly. She reviewed the off-campus work that he was participating in on Mondays, Wednesdays, and Fridays, noting how disappointed he was when he couldn't go out to "work." This job was at a restaurant, where he refilled items on the tables and performed other small tasks before they opened in the morning. One year after this meeting, he lost the job because of a bipolar outburst. [Author's note: To this point, Ben has never had another job in the community, though he has chores at his home.]

Following Ben's direction, we turned our attention next to the person sitting to my left—the director, Jill. She clarified her plan for when Ben exhibited an unwanted behavior: he would come to "talk" to her, sitting on a special chair in the hall by her office. "After we talk about his disappointment, he is easily diverted and eager to go back to his room again."

Frances, Eric, and Sandy noted the decrease in Ben's anxiety medication after his first full year in the day program. We all remembered *our* many anxieties of one year ago. Right from the beginning, I had wondered if Jill was exhibiting an extra bravado, or if she genuinely refused to expect the worst. Jill never gave in to our fears. I believe she fully expected minimal problems.

Her quiet professionalism comforted me again as she smiled at Ben and acknowledged the success she'd expected. Her calm, in-control demeanor may well have been part of the reason the center exuded peace, even amid the apparent chaos of its clients.

This day program at the adult activity center, among the most celebrated in Michigan and around the country, was closed on short notice just a few years later, when state and federal agencies pulled its funding. All across the nation, special needs adults lost day programs, and organizations like MOKA—and their staff—had to pick up the slack.

Putting up two fingers behind Eric's head, grinning, Ben tickled his way up to Eric's shoulder, receiving a ferocious response from Eric's teeth, which set off squeals of delight and conspiratorial camaraderie. This behavior continued through most of the meeting. PCP meeting? Nope. "Ben-centered party" was a better definition this time!

When I first met Ben's flamboyant psychologist, I truthfully only really noticed her *many* pairs of stylish glasses and her admitted obsession with shoes and accessories. I had immediately disliked her when she insisted we should treat my eighteen-year-old boy according to his chronological age. I felt he was more of a three-year-old thrown into boot camp at that time, as my readers know! I believed she had to learn compassion. And yes, I also had much to learn about letting go of my maternal role!

She eagerly reported how she had shampooed and massaged Ben's head the week before when she made an early morning visit, and how much he had liked it. She also revisited how Ben had choked her during the early, turbulent years of his adult life, but quickly noted that Ben still signed "sorry" to her every time he saw her. Her love and compassion were representative of every person at that table. We reviewed our hopes for fewer outbursts overall, but we were pleased with his many improvements. One big improvement? I had learned to appreciate and even like his psychologist!

She and Eric noted how the men in the home acted like siblings. Part of the team shared memories of an infamous late-night meeting, which had begun around nine o'clock in the evening on the previous Wednesday. They'd quickly come together over the urgent need to remove one of those siblings from Ben's home. The opening I mentioned earlier had become available, and they all needed to consult together to determine the best course of action. The meeting lasted well into the night, and the result was the new, calm atmosphere in the tiny structure that housed as many as six men for too long.

Deb, Ben's speech therapist, gave her update next. She said he had begun using five new signs since last year—but none of them could remember which ones at that moment! Though I'd seen him use many of the signs, Ben was not going to show us right then either. He wasn't working today, he seemed to say, as he hid his face in his hands. "Okay, Ben, you're right. This isn't program time!"

Years before we had hoped Ben might learn to communicate with Augmentative and alterative communication methods. But, after many attempts at training him to select pictures that would enable the gadget to voice the related word, he only used it as a game. He would repeatedly hit the same picture, but not choose on his own. Officially, we removed the GoTalk computer device from his care plan.

We all agreed that signing and gestures worked best for Ben. We added five new signs for things he needed or used every day. Learning them became some of Ben's goals for the next year.

I was encouraged as the team members described "knowing" what Ben needed. They *understood* what he communicated to them. Eric—between comical glares at Ben and more snapping—noted that he had added "Ben language" to his resumé!

We ended the ninety-minute meeting with my traditional thanks to all of them, reminding them how much Ed and I appreciated their labor and love for Ben. I assured them that I felt my most important job in all of this was to pray, and that I took it seriously!

Ben already knew we were going to lunch, so we got in the car and I let him choose: McDonald's? Burger King? Wendy's? Bob Evans? He gave several definitive grunts and pointed a finger off to the right. "You sure, Ben?" I asked as we drew near to Bob Evans. I was glad. Of all the restaurants he liked, I knew I could most easily make a soft, mashed meal from their menu, for his special dietary needs.

We parked, and Ben reached for my hand, eagerly walking me in. From their photo menu (I love this, people!), he selected a strawberry fruit smoothie and scrambled eggs. We split a peach cobbler à la mode for dessert, all blended.

As we climbed back in the car, I explained again, "No, Ben, no house today. You were home two days ago! Did we play ball? Yes! Today you're heading back to work!"

Ben did great, I thought, saying a warm hi to Frances when we got back to the center. His housemate, Orion, eagerly greeted him. After greeting others in the room, I left, feeling satisfied with our time together. Just as I turned the key, though, Ben walked out to the car, signing "House?"

I rolled down the window. "Nope. Come and give me a kiss, buddy!" He did. Waving goodbye, then, with his right hand in the air, bending his fingers at the middle knuckle, he moved to take a seat next to his friend on the outdoor glider. He was smiling.

That was the last time I brought Ben to the center or visited there. I learned afterward that his severe separation anxiety made our parting very dangerous for the staff.

I had meant well.

CHAPTER 24

Can We Just Start Over?

All is not well

All week, my thoughts never strayed far from Sunday's trauma. Opening the second drawer of our metal file cabinet, I dug through the thickest, dog-eared bin, overflowing with bulletin flyers, yellowed notebook pages, and construction paper—all of Ben's drawings. I was certain there must be something in there that could describe this time. I found one drawing that felt perfect.

We had been eager to have Ben with us in church again. It had been quite a while. Around 8:50 a.m., a big gray van pulled into our yard. Ginger, one of the aides we loved so much, was the driver.

Housemate Craig always jumped out first and extended his hand as if he were the landowner only come to inspect the farm. I shook his hand. "Hi, Craig. How's it going?'"

"Where are your goats?"

"We haven't had goats in a long time!"

Shifting his glasses up a little on his narrow nose, he pointed toward the barn. "There's a cat."

"Yup, that's Pumpkin."

Ben had climbed out now, maneuvering his 250-pound frame from his seat in the back of the twelve-passenger van. With an eager grin, he gave us his giant, warm hug, proudly showing me his close shave.

"Mmmm, you smell nice, Ben. And *wow!* Your face feels great!"

He beamed.

Then—our only hint that things were a little shaky—Ginger said, "He wouldn't let me brush his teeth this morning, so you may want to."

After a few more hints that he wanted to come to the farm again soon, Craig reluctantly climbed back in the van. Ben realized they were leaving and gave Ginger a tender hug, placing a wet kiss on her cheek. She turned the van toward the morning sun and headed home.

[Note: Craig was an excellent housemate for Ben. He welcomed Ben enthusiastically and became Ben's voice at times. A great pal! He made Ben's life more fun and helped the staff with many little details. He had heart issues and died one night very suddenly. We still miss him!]

Ben giggled and choked as Dad playfully brushed his teeth, then reminded me of what was to come by turning his right hand on his left palm in the motion of a cookie cutter. Coffee time in the fellowship hall was what Ben most liked about church.

"Yup, there'll be cookies and lots of people," I assured him. "Remember to be good."

During the church service, he leaned toward me, inquisitive, periodically kissing my cheek. After about ten minutes of the sermon, he started signing, "Pray."

"Not yet, Ben, sshh," I whispered.

Then came the sign for "cookie."

"Pretty soon," I promised.

As the sermon grew much longer, he looked at me a little desperately, signing "pray" again, meaning "sermon done."

"Do you want to go out with me, Ben?" I asked with a smile.

He shook his head, not sure of himself.

Finally, we began communion. He let me select the tiny plastic juice glass out of the brassy tray. I gingerly put it in his big hand, and he gulped it down with the rest of us. Getting his attention, I kissed my fingertips, then touched each palm with my middle finger, signing "Thank you, Jesus."

"Jesus loves Ben," I added out loud, praying as I often did that Jesus would give him that assurance.

As soon as we hit the aisle, he latched on to a gentleman who responded lovingly to Ben's characteristic outburst of affection. Ben barrelled through the hall, with me restraining his speed. I pushed a seat against a wall in the fellowship hall to get him seated, not prowling for more cookies … or babies. I thought, *We can never relax around babies!*

Usually, the children walked along the other hall directly to their Sunday school classrooms. But, unknown to me, this was a very special Sunday. All the children, kindergarten through fifth grade, flooded into the fellowship hall for a missionary program.

They noticed Ben then and began giggling and playing the shooting game with him. "Pickew," they would shout, then fall when Ben shot them back. They laughed and played more and more boldly with him. I tried to control it, standing at his knee—ready, I thought.

My six-year-old friend Maddie came up for her usual hug, then said, "I don't know this boy, do I?"

"Well, Maddie, this is our big son Ben. He loves to play."

She started falling in front of his pistol excitedly then, and invited others to join her. Spontaneously, before I could stop her, she gave him her characteristically warm six-year-old hug and returned to her play.

In that same moment, our youth pastor's wife stepped up, holding her baby on her hip. Purposefully taking another step toward Ben, she chirped, "Hi, Ben!" Before I could stop her forward motion, Ben grabbed two-year-old Noah's arm and tightened his grip.

Instead of staying calm, which is *always* better with Ben, I let out a reactionary yell for him to let go. Desperately I tried to peel his fingers off while struggling to gain my composure for the sake of Noah and the other children.

Ed had seen Ben's eyes change from playful to hard, which often signaled the rise of the no-longer-dormant bipolar monster. He, too, had quickly moved forward, but couldn't stop what came next.

Somehow I freed Noah. But, forcefully, Ben grabbed a bunch of my hair instead and pulled my head into his lap. In a seizure-like movement, he sank his teeth into my scalp, keeping me in that vise lock for over five minutes.

I could hear Ed's firm voice pleading with Ben. Remembering some advice from a policeman friend of ours, Ed started applying pressure to a specific area of Ben's neck. Our friend had assured Ed it would incapacitate a strong man. It did nothing. Ed later said he used other "foolproof"—and painful—techniques for getting Ben to release, to no avail.

Meanwhile, Ben was wailing, a horrible sound that said, "Help me! I don't want to do this! Help me!" (At least, that's my spirit's interpretation.) Saliva drooled from his mouth. Tears sprang from his eyes and animalistic growls and grunts rose from his soul. But his strength was not diminished.

As I stood with my head upside down, hair locked between his fingers, his teeth in my scalp, I saw children and a woman off to my side, standing there stunned. The woman later assured me she'd been praying, reminded of hard times she'd experienced with her father who had Alzheimer's. Looking back, I remembered how many people had been there praying, and I was comforted.

But at the time, I pleaded, "Go away!" I yelled, sobbing between my gasps of pain and embarrassment—for Ben and for me. Most of these people had never seen anything but laughter, hugs, and smiles from Ben. *What are those children thinking about their friend from a moment before?* "Oh, God!" I groaned over and over, struggling to get free. "Please don't let people think poorly about Ben," I begged from the depths of my soul.

Suddenly I was freed, my whole body shaking uncontrollably. My blood sugar dived during the extended expenditure of energy and emotion after the long church service. I grabbed my purse and popped a glucose tablet in my mouth while tearing open a little envelope that held Ben's sedatives. I ran to the kitchen window to get water for Ben. The poor gal had no idea what I needed and tried to get *cold* water. "Just water!" I shrieked.

I forced Ben to take the pill while Ed and another man held his arms. He wouldn't or couldn't swallow, so the tablet threatened to fall out of his mouth with his saliva. I positioned myself behind him, grabbing his chin as he tried to bite the men holding him. Though his teeth were chomping, I made him drink and swallow again, praying against his danger of choking from aspiration.

Finally, Ben began to relax. The adults had taken the children out of the hall. Many people offered help. Some volunteered to ride with us while we helped our overwrought son through the doors and to the van. Ben was meeker, but still striking out unexpectedly. We asked him to please sit in the seat furthest to the back. Thankfully he agreed, whimpering and wailing intermittently, reaching out, supposedly to hug me.

I moved to the back hatch and opened it, thinking I would buckle him in from behind. Immediately losing another fistful of hair. I gave the door a heave and stumbled to my passenger seat. We thanked the men, acknowledging their desire to help, but all we wanted to do was leave that scene!

Silently, we drove to Ben's home, thirty miles away. We were alert every minute, ready to respond as quickly as possible, if necessary. I phoned to update the staff in cryptic language. Plans for dinner and fun with Ben at our home were gone. Silently we prayed he would stay in his seat for the whole trip.

I couldn't stop wondering, *Ever? Can we ever do this again? Can we just start this day over?* Waves of sorrow and nausea kept washing over me. I worked to hide my emotions from Ben, who kept holding out his arms, sobbing "Muhmuh!" The effects of the sedative were progressing.

Thoughts of James and Aubrey and the tremendous embarrassment they might have suffered made me physically sick. James would have been fifteen at that point, and Aubrey probably seventeen. She usually drove the two of them to church.

James is very introspective. Even today, as a grown man in the army, he recoils from drama or unnecessary attention. He never draws attention to himself and walks away from emotional rants. He doesn't like the attitude of soldiers who complain about standard work or draw attention to themselves, rather than putting their heads and hands to the task and being part of the squad. I often prayed that God would heal these siblings from the many challenging scenes that accompanied their growing-up years. I believe God has used each hard thing in their lives to grow their characters.

When we got to Ben's house, I jumped out before the van completely stopped, so that Ben couldn't strike me on his way out. I felt he was back under control, but I did not dare give him a parting hug when he held out his hands to me. Ed kept his distance too, guardedly walking Ben in.

All that day a horrible weight chained us in place, defying the sunshine outside. Sorrow gripped our hearts and taunted us back into the dark despair we knew too well—reminding us of all we longed for and things we would never know with Ben on this earth.

Late that night, trying to find sleep, I felt my big, strong husband's body begin to shake. I held my gentle mate closer. He finally rasped, "It's just so unnatural to hurt your son!"

"Can we just start over?" I'd labeled this picture. I thought I would use it when I told the story about trying to get Ben dressed. Now I knew where it really fit in his story. All through that day and next morning, that and other questions tormented me. *Should we have left and not let any of the kids play with Ben? What if he'd hurt my Maddie? Alex? Any number of innocent, loving, laughing children?*

I called the young pastor to check on Noah. Noah was perfectly fine, he very gracefully said. Just two weeks prior, we'd had another incident with a baby in that young pastor's home—a second episode after more than a year of trustworthy behavior. We had been lulled into thinking Ben could visit people he loved.

I had to take ownership of my desire to include Ben in our lives. It was always a question of inclusion versus safe boundaries.

Unbidden, memories of the months surrounding Ben's eighteenth birthday returned. For months, we got calls several times a week regarding Ben's new, erratic, violent behaviors. For the first time in our lives, we could relate to parents who waited, sleepless, at night, wondering if their phone would ring or if a police car would appear in their driveway. I squeezed back the memory of the day our other children found the courage to tell us they were not safe. Ben had terrorized them—I hoped—for the last time.

God, help! Can we just start over? The answer was clearly no. *God! Why did that have to happen, and so publicly?* I shuddered at the mental image of people talking to others, probably right then. The only thing that came close to giving me an answer was the fact that people who loved Ben and who loved us now knew a little more about Ben. They had been front-row spectators to the horrible and ugly aspects of his disabilities.

Our senior pastor called on Monday morning. They'd prayed for us at the staff meeting that morning, and he wanted us to know that. He asked if we were all right. "No," I choked, tears flowing immediately. Truthfully, I admitted, "It will be a little while before we're all right again."

He heard my sorrow and assured us they didn't think anything negative about Ben. In fact, he said, if there was anything good about it, they had used that valuable opportunity to talk with their children about people with special needs. His love and concern were an answer to our prayer.

Later that week, I received a surprising note from a young mom from church who had a child with autism. She'd never known we had a special needs child, nor why I had empathized with her lack of sleep and her struggles. She said she now felt she wasn't alone.

As I told our pastor, the ache doesn't just go away. Like so many other families, we have a child with a rough diagnosis. We keep babies from Ben, unless it's a controlled environment. Ben has been absent from extended family gatherings now for many years. By God's grace many of Ben's aides have taken their babies to work or freely let him handle their children—under supervision of course. He also enjoys volunteering at a local animal shelter over the last year or so, and gets to interact with dogs and cats, and loves it!

In years past, from the fall season straight through March was awful for Ben. The year prior, it had been great. We had let our guard down. Since that incident, we have never taken him back to church. The setting is just too unregulated.

But that's the thing with a bipolar diagnosis: there are seasons, patterns, prescription complications, good days, and bad days. Good seasons like the one we'd experienced, followed by really, really bad ones.

And yet I could begin to see a possible yes to my question, "Can we just start over?" Regarding *future* fears of any kind, we could start over with God's promises: forgiveness for something Ben cannot control, mercy for the sadness he feels, and grace for those who judge unknowingly.

It's the same way God deals with me: forgiveness, mercy, and grace, fresh each day. Could I trust God to turn even this horrific event into a "good thing," as he promised? Do "all things" really "work together for good to those who love him"? Romans 8:28 (KJV)

These are the facts: Ed and I have a son, our children have a brother, and our grandchildren have an uncle who is unique. We have a grown son: a handsome man who still, after all these years, causes us and himself an enormous amount of emotional pain and suffering. Could our brothers and sisters be trusted with this fact and still not judge us—or the son we love? Could grace be that big?

The only answer I found for myself, came directly from communion—the communion we had shared that day! That is where I fully understand and acknowledge the depths of God's love for all of us and the enormity of my own incapacities and shortcomings. I don't have to wonder. I know and I trust that God is able. *Can we just start over*? **Yes**! That is exactly what "redemption" means. He took an ugly cross and redeemed a whole world. He took ashes and gave beauty in their place. Isn't that what we proclaim in communion? All is not well in any of our lives. We need a Redeemer!

That "yes" above comes from my good friend, Gail MacDonald's influence. Often in her talks with Pastors' Wives at gatherings around the country, I stayed in the room, after leading in worship—privileged to hear her speak from her heart, and from her life's experience. She would often use the encouragement to live life to the full—live free of shackles from the past—say **yes**! to all that God has for us. She lives that way, and I want to too, especially with the mental illness Ben continually brings to our family.

Because of Christ, I live in hope, knowing that we share, in a little part, the suffering of Christ. I gratefully sip from that cup of anguish with my son. As I figuratively try to hide Ben behind a protective covering or lead him to a safer spot, I remember another who showed us how to serve. And we do. Just start over.

CHAPTER 25

Bowling

He boogied for superior effect

One evening, all the kids and I decided to take Ben out for a night of bowling. It is the one sport Ben has had years of practice in, and we all were a little afraid we'd be embarrassed by his score. We were almost right!

Three of our other children and I arrived at Ben's home just after supper. He had been patiently sitting at the dining table for an hour. Jumping up and doing a jig as we entered, he self-consciously brushed his face with his hands to hide his nervous excitement. He shouted as he climbed into the front passenger seat after catching sight of the van full of siblings,

His excitement mounted as I asked him where to go. "Do I turn here? Here? Where *is* that bowling alley?" I asked as we drove the three miles to the alley. He knew exactly where to go and proudly pointed off to the right at the proper time. "There? Really?" I asked. "Are you sure?"

"Yaaaah," he droned, in his slightly patronizing voice. He loves this finding game. Persistently, he pointed in his whole-hand way, to the right, looking a little perturbed by the delay.

"Okay," I said and pretended to drive right past the driveway.

'Uhhhh!" he gasped as I made an abrupt turn to the right. Falling toward me, he searched madly for the over-the-door grab handle, trying to keep his balance, weak with giggling. His siblings were not giggling, assessing how many people were watching my crazy driving, afraid of how the van was appearing and of what I might yet do.

I couldn't resist. Every time Ben is in the car with me, I have the urge to give him a carnival ride.

"Look out!" I yelled, and careened through the *nearly* empty parking lot, swerving and circling to the right, then the left. Ben's chortling spurred me on. "This isn't it! Ben, we're lost!" As he caught his breath, he pointed weakly, persistently, to the building right in front of us. "Are you sure?"

"Yaaaaah!"

"Okay, ready for bowling?"

"Yaaaah!"

As we walked up the indoor ramp, I noticed the glass case that displayed bowling shoes, a bowling ball bag, and shirts. It is always hard to find gifts that are perfect for Ben. I made a mental note and went in, making sure I held the door for his tipsy bulk.

I searched for a wildly painted ball for Ben as the others picked out their own weights. I actually love bowling, even though I probably haven't done it more than fifteen times in my life. I was eager for the playtime!

I wasn't sure what size ball Ben used when he bowled. Not to worry! He corrected us with hands out and a stern "Uh-uh!" if it looked like we were going to pick up the wrong ball. *He* selected and picked up the ball he wanted in two hands, then sauntered down the alley to our lane.

Looking like he wasn't paying any attention, he threw the ball right down the middle almost every time, invariably hitting six or seven pins with each throw—and even an occasional strike!

He had his bowling game down, obviously, but keeping his backside covered was the real challenge. He had developed an enormous stomach at that time, and his pants slipped off the waist and sagged beneath the middle. That meant that every time he sat down, his pants followed the natural bend of his knees—down and out. Likewise, every time he stood up, we were alert to the flash. We didn't catch him every single time, and finally the giggles took over. He thought we were laughing at his walk, so he boogied for superior effect.

We were reminded again that his trainer, Bob, had done a thorough job of teaching Ben to follow a pattern when he bowled. Those years of training ensured that Ben would have an enjoyable, lifetime social game skill. Without seeming to know where he was looking or what his gauge was, he threw the ball right down the middle of the lane effortlessly. He didn't grip with fingers in the holes, but with both hands around the enormously heavy ball (if you believed Ben's exaggerated efforts and grunts each time he lifted it off the return).

By the sixth frame, our youngest son James was getting thoroughly discouraged. He had only played this sport one or two times before at that time, so gutter balls were a dime a dozen for him that day. Ben didn't mean to, but he was demoralizing James without even using the finger holes!

As usual, Ben had my attention. I was most interested in making sure he was having a good time, congratulating him on each toss. I should have prepared his younger brother for the competition! James threw the ball for the last time—into the gutter, limping to a seat off to the side, totally dejected.

As usual, Ben's antennae picked up on it. For the next three frames, he acted progressively sillier, drawing attention to himself.

"Okay, Ben, show us what ya got!" we called.

He walked down the lane the same way he'd done in each preceding frame, clowning around and looking like he didn't care where the ball landed. But in these frames, each throw landed the ball in the gutter. He would turn around, slap his leg, shake his head from left to right, and cover his open mouth with his hand.

"Ben! What happened?" we asked sympathetically. He turned on his dejected face. Then, coming to sit down, tried to catch James's eye.

Ben spent many years antagonizing James, at the dinner table and in many more situations. I love this one solid memory of Ben having compassion on James, trying to help <u>him</u> feel better.

On Christmas Day a few months later, Ben squealed with delight when he opened a heavy box, revealing a shiny black ball covered in yellow smiley emojis, a bowling bag…and an *extra long* bowling shirt.

In 2011, Ben first met Jen's boyfriend, Kelvin Miller. I wondered—we all wondered—how the first meeting would go. We arranged a no-fuss bonfire, and Ben's first reaction on their very first meeting was a bear hug. Jenny was pretty happy with Ben's acceptance of the man she was falling in love with.

Kelvin is the oldest sibling in his birth family. And he has a younger brother with special needs. He is a fabulous addition to our family—a safety officer and a firefighter for the township where he and Jen built their home, and a wonderful father!

It turned out that Kelvin liked bowling and was the best at it of all of us. *That* was why he is a very important part of this story. Jen and Kelvin were married eight months later. Good job, Ben!

James didn't have to compete with Ben on any other playing field. If Ben knew how often James gets to shoot real guns at a range, or saw James deploying a drone as a specialist, Ben would be the one who would be totally dejected.

This picture shows James wearing a new patch for Skeeter, the cartoon-like mascot James drew up and painted on the wing of an army drone he works with. In fact, the whole platoon is now called the Skeeter Platoon after the name James picked for it! Ben isn't the only artist in the family!

Recently I asked James if he would write a few words about his relationship to Ben. He was reticent to go public, but I'm thankful he put the following into writing. I think it represents how a lot of men feel about disabilities in their family.

"I didn't grow up with Ben, as Rachel and Jen did, so I missed out on a lot of experiences and learning his personality from a young age. But I did grow up with Aubrey, who has always been a good friend to Ben and a wonderful sister to both of us. Aubrey has taught me how to love Ben when I can't understand him or figure out why some days he is just not easy to get along with. She always seems to know what to say to Ben, whether it's bringing him back in line or exclaiming how good his haircut looks.

When I think of my relationship with Ben, the memories that I associate with him, they're mostly unpleasant. It's the times that he would be violent at home, or at 'his house' that stick with me the most.

I often think of his disabilities physically, I hate that he can't walk with ease, I hate that he falls and his brain doesn't know why. I want him to get better every time I see him, knowing it won't happen on this Earth. It's weird being the 'little brother' to Ben; we both know he's the first born, the big brother but I think we both feel the tension. I'm younger but I have to be the protector and everything else a big brother is supposed to be, I hold his hand as he climbs stairs, or goes to the car in the snow. Those are things no man in his twenties or thirties would want to be that way.

Although I love his spirit, he knows I don't trust his body because of how many times it has betrayed him and hurt himself or other people seemingly out of the blue. That is something I have had in the back of my mind for a long time, that I want to be a road block between his rare bipolar outbursts or lack of balance and those who are in the area. It's not a comfortable relationship, I don't know if that's possible with Ben, but I feel we both love each other, it's hard enough as a man making friends with other men, harder with a brotherly relationship when neither can explain the distance between.

Ben's brighter side wins 90% of the time, so I don't know why the heavy situations stay in my mind so much clearer. His laugh is infectious, his sense of humor is similar to mine, we both love animated children's movies and action films, and I think we both want to be the hero and defender. I love that he loves art, and he pursues it as well as he can.

Even when he's being facetious he will bring smiles to strangers and friends faces, something I certainly don't do, which makes me smile just thinking about him poking someone with a scowl, declaring "bubbee," and turning away. Exactly what I want to do to people sometimes."

CHAPTER 26

Sister Number Three

Learn before judging, and love before dismissing

When Aubrey was in college, she wrote a paper about Ben. The final paragraph is an excellent depiction of her current relationship with Ben:

I have learned more from my older brother than I ever will from anyone else. He has taught me to love unconditionally by giving hugs to those who, without knowing the struggles he's gone through, judge and laugh at him. Ben ironically teaches me patience by being impatient at the dinner table. I'm shown how to say hello by his bear hugs, sloppy kisses, and loud "Hi!" I was taught how to dance by the silly moves he'll make when his favorite song comes on the radio. I know to be myself at all times because Ben isn't afraid to be himself. He taught me how to ask for forgiveness by the giant tears that roll down his face because of his regret. Life with Ben can be difficult, but it's also incredibly rewarding, and I wouldn't have it any other way.

"Aubee" (Ben's coveted name for Aubrey—the only one he comes close to pronouncing) was born one month before Ben turned ten years old. She was only eight years old when Ben entered adult foster care. Since growing up, she's made some beautiful memories with Ben, but the fact remains that all our children's lives were affected by Ben, and not always positively. Aubrey once said she didn't have any happy memories of Ben when he lived at home. We began the process of looking for alternative housing for Ben when we found our children—including Aubrey—were locking themselves in their bedrooms or the bathroom when left with Ben.

Today, Aubrey is a Certified Therapeutic Recreation Specialist and is currently ('18-'19) getting a masters degree. She's also certified through PATH International in therapeutic riding, using horses for therapy with people who have physical, cognitive, or emotional struggles or disabilities.

The following is also an article she wrote, while a student at Calvin College. She used it as the base for a talk she gave to people who specifically cared for siblings of special needs persons. As a sibling herself, she does a good job of asking (and answering) some pretty key questions. I hope you'll find it helpful in your journey.

I was silent about both the struggles my family endured as well as the laughter my brother Ben brought to our lives until my first year of college. Having an older brother with severe developmental disabilities meant my life looked very different from my classmates, classmates who didn't understand limitations first hand. I vividly remember an event where a change in routine caused a flip to switch in my brother that he couldn't control. He was attending my sporting event with our parents, and at 6'3" and well over 200 lbs., his outburst was dangerous, intimidating, and I'm sure confusing for the many bystanders.

When faced with questions from friends, I remember feeling so torn. I didn't know how to be honest about the frustrating and sometimes scary reality of life with Ben, while at the same time communicating that he was, still is, and always would be, the older brother I loved dearly and couldn't imagine life without. Explaining the frequent ugliness of his diagnosis seemed like a betrayal to a brother who I knew would feel great remorse for his uncontrollable actions a couple of hours later.

It wasn't until I realized that I could be a voice for Ben that I opened up. Now, after a few years of discussions and reflection, I would like to offer some insight on what was helpful growing up, what would have been helpful, and what I need now, as an adult.

What Was Helpful

For the last 25+ years, a friend of our family has prayed for Ben every Tuesday (and still does). He called my parents often for updates, and would always call or visit on Ben's birthday as well as send a card, usually with a gift. Knowing that someone besides a family member truly cared for Ben was and is encouraging and uplifting.

When I was nearing the end of high school, my church got a new youth pastor, whose wife had a sister very similar to Ben. Being able to talk about some of the hard things as well as the joys made processing more comfortable and brought a connection different than others I had while growing up.

What Would Have Been Helpful

A Support group: A support group with peers who had similar experiences and whose feelings I could relate to, would have been incredibly therapeutic. I think having a safe place to talk about my disappointments and fears that otherwise stayed secret would have decreased my feelings of being alone and different. It would have also been wonderful to share the joyful moments, which often felt small compared to some of the negatives, with others who understood.

Professional counseling: Along with a support group, it might have been helpful to go to professional counseling. I didn't receive any until last year, and now that I've been able to talk through it with a counselor, I wish I could have attended earlier in life.

Openness: Openness within my family would have allowed me to process the highs and lows as well. I know my parents wanted to shield me from the difficulties as much as they could, and although I am grateful for their wisdom, I am even more thankful for the times we are now able to talk openly about the hard times. A family goes through many highs and lows together. As painful as it is to talk about the "hard stuff," such as the wishes and dreams that are desired for the sibling that won't be reached, it's important to uncover those hurts. It's also vital to talk about the delight the sibling brings to the family, as it can be easy to overlook the gift of being blessed with a sibling with disabilities. I've learned more about life from Ben than from any other person.

Genuine Interest: Something I have always wanted is the ability to know if those who asked questions were genuinely interested in knowing who Ben was as an individual. I would have felt much more comfortable talking to people about the joys and hardships if I knew they were willing to learn before judging, and love before dismissing.

All of the above are still needed and greatly appreciated. With the blessing and challenge of a sibling with disabilities comes a need for openness, honesty, and a network of support. After realizing how I can be an even greater part of Ben's life, I have a different perspective on who I am as Ben's little sister than I did growing up. I still have torn feelings when asked hard questions, but I understand now that I, along with my family members and those close to Ben, can be the voice he doesn't have. Join a Sibling Support Group!

CHAPTER 27

Questions You Might Have

Adult Foster Care? No Way!

This chapter began as a talk I was asked to give at a banquet, both connecting special needs families with one another and hosting representatives from community support organizations. I think there are significant issues mentioned here that may be helpful for those who wonder how to get help for a family member with special needs. Many adults have a high-functioning disability and may only need support to be able to live on their own or to enjoy social settings. These services are available in many communities. Some of you may also be wondering what adult foster care would look like for your family member. Here are a few things I've learned on this journey.

First of all, I hope prayer will be the beginning of your search for information and help regarding your loved one. I could never say enough about the depth of spiritual and practical guidance that has come to me from God over these many years, in answer to prayer.

Then, use any medical or psychological diagnosis your loved one has, along with their associated websites and specialists within that field. There are many organizations listed in cyberspace, along with phone numbers that will help you begin. The website disabilityscoop.com (https:// disabilityscoop.com) is full of relevant information and will lead to other relevant sites. Denial is not usually a good option!

I receive mailings now from local organizations that have legislative information and form committees to keep us abreast of things happening that can impact Ben's services. At one meeting several months ago, we learned of relevant local legislative changes secondary to changes in Federal funding. These will profoundly affect the services our loved ones enjoy. We have to be prepared when we can, and not live in denial or ignorance.

If you had asked me before Ben's eighteenth birthday how I felt about adult foster care for Ben, I would have said emphatically, "No way!" We assumed Ben would always live with us, and we planned for it. But in 2001, a behavioral home became our only option for his care. That step had to begin by doing the legwork of becoming Ben's legal guardians—at least in Michigan. Otherwise he would have automatically become a ward of the state.

It's not hard to tell, if you read any of the previous chapters, that I was grief-stricken—like many of you who have had to go through trying days and years. I wondered how strangers could ever know Ben's needs. His speech was and is almost nonexistent. He needs twenty-four-hour staffing. Who would ever take care of him as we did? Given his severe attachment disorder, how would he ever detach from the family he adored?

That first AFC home was not deserving of our son, nor the money they received from the state for his care. I didn't know how to attempt a formal complaint, but I did my best, reporting on four situations that compromised Ben's safety and broke their contract. Thankfully, they eventually lost their license—after a better home opened for Ben—but their operations ended, and no one else would be made to suffer there. Do the best you can do!

May I encourage you with an insight I had several years after Ben left our home? I thought I was the connector for Ben—the person who introduced him to new people and new situations in his life. I thought everything about his life had to go through my fingers of control and protection, and I believed my thought process was of value to Ben.

It was a revelation to me to realize that Ben himself would make his way. While he could never live on his own, he would become a blessing to people I may never meet. That was more than good enough for me. God had a plan for Ben's life. Just as it is for my other adult children, that plan is Ben's alone. It doesn't include me. And that's pretty awesome.

What Are Behavioral Homes?

I probably wouldn't know that behavioral homes exist if it weren't for Ben. A behavioral adult foster care home is a continuation of one of the services offered by Community Mental Health, providing integrated healthcare for individuals living with serious and persistent mental illness.

Now, almost two decades after his initial placement, I can say more knowledgeably, what a tremendous blessing the MOKA organization has been to our family. MOKA is a privately held organization, working in conjunction with CMH. Because of Ben's psychological and mental needs, I've been privileged to meet the best of people—servant-hearted individuals with a passion for investing in the lives of those who could never live on their own.

I suspect such professionals rarely stay if the paycheck is their only incentive. Our local MOKA organization, and CMH has confirmed that great personnel have left for menial jobs with comparable pay because those jobs don't have any of the stress and responsibility AFC homes have. The MOKA.org home page reads, "MOKA was developed to enhance the full inclusion of individuals with disabilities into our communities." This was our hope for Ben.

What Do Adult Foster Homes Look Like?

It takes many people to make one AFC home run efficiently: a hard-working supervisor (a person of integrity), along with oversight from the Department of Health and Human Services, Community Mental Health (CMH). In Ben's case—and probably in all the behavioral homes, aides work on three shifts and through most holidays: washing bodies when needed, washing dishes, and washing clothes. In recent years, daily activities like arts, crafts, and community outings have been added, since all the CMH day programs in Michigan—and most, across the country were closed in 2016.

The home staff keep track of doctors' appointments, family connections, and simpler things like haircuts—even noting which hairdresser is best for each man. Ben *loves* the hot towel and neck massage included in the haircut and offers no resistance. Giving him a haircut was part of the worst times with Ben when he was a child. To say he squirmed is an understatement not to be compared with the battle he engaged in with the mere sight of scissors!

I marvel at the freedom Ben enjoys today and the incredible support he has, which makes his adult life full of accomplishments, relationships, and meaning. Ed and I and Ben's siblings are chiefly grateful for the staff's respect for Ben. We appreciate all the ways they make his life orderly and rewarding.

What Kind of People Work for These Organizations?

In adult foster care, there are women and men on the staff—the balance, sadly weighted more to women in Ben's home, though we have had remarkable men, young and old. This, though, is dependent on the requirements of each guardian. My friend, Deb, usually insisted that their daughter have only female staff until recently. That may be a legal requirement in some homes. We have had college-age people who were working their way through school and wondering if a career working with our population might be in their future. There have been women, men, and grandmas, along with people in their twenties. There are tests they need to pass, and certainly have a clean criminal record.

Ben's staff keeps busy distracting residents from negative behaviors, cleaning behind those who cannot clean themselves, and listening to their stories. They encourage healthy decisions and plan outings. They attend in-service training, which is needed to keep up with laws and care techniques vital to the safety and well-being of our loved ones. Some homes run with only one or two staff who don't even have to be there overnight, dependent on the client and their level of self sufficiency.

If you are dealing with behavioral issues, there is one crucial program you will want to be aware of: Gentle Teaching International (https://gti2018.nl/en/). It has meant a great deal to us as we see how it affects responses to Ben's behaviors.

The house Ben lives in is homey and comfortable. It was pleasant and warm when it was small and had plumbing problems. It is the same now that it is luxuriously large.

For seven years, I traveled three times a year for four-day events around the country in my work as a worship leader with Focus on the Family. I had many opportunities to meet with moms of special needs individuals in breakout sessions. I was surprised at the wide disparity from one state to another in the level and kinds of supports available.

West Michigan has a rich history of people seeing the need and taking steps to change lives. The level of care that Ben receives speaks to the caliber of people at the many great, caring organizations in this state. It is a tribute to the faith and hard work that planned and grew such outstanding organizations, and the generosity that keeps caring corporations and foundations operating and accountable today. I'm not naive enough to think there is unlimited funding available. I encourage the generosity of businesses and individuals who become aware of the need to become involved.

If you need to look at the adult foster care option, what should you expect from a home supervisor? I literally didn't know anything. But Ben's supervisor (then Eric) was a hands-on manager. Eric had coffee with the men in the morning and popped in day and night, making sure staff were accountable for their actions to him and the clients he represented. Each staff person was responsible for reporting any incidents that endangered Ben or the others in that home. They were also accountable to report on a fellow employee if they witnessed something untoward. I would also receive an incident report from Community Mental Health, even if I didn't hear about it firsthand from Eric.

Eric always referred to the AFC house as "their home." He worked at making it home, and led his team in being careful with the resources they received, recognizing those resources as a trust from a generous community.

I have mentioned Eric repeatedly because of his track record of over twenty years as a home supervisor. He left the teaching profession, choosing to work with men like Ben to make a difference in their lives. He taught his staff and many others how to love and respect the residents. They now carry on his legacy.

Even though that house was small, Ben immediately began to thrive on the love and respect he was given. On many occasions, Ben was a guest of Eric and his hospitable wife Becky, especially enjoying the many rescued dogs at their home. Ben has been a guest in the homes of many staff members on the team that we have so grown to love. The staff include the men in their holiday outings if we can't make a plan with Ben.

Today, Ben has a wonderful supervisor in Janessa. She has sent text messages with pictures of big events in Ben's life, and when I've mentioned concerns they are usually addressed very promptly. During the last IEPC meeting, I was amazed at the amount of personal touches she accepted in her personal space, specifically her face, from one of Ben's housemates. I would not have been able to keep my control for that long without just moving into another area, or asking him to stop, please!

Will There Be Room for Personal Preferences?

If it's important to Ben, the staff will—and should—do whatever they can to facilitate it. You want that! Some of their activities include winter bowling outings, shopping, worship, feeding ducks at the beach, and eating at a favorite restaurant. Ben chooses his favorite videos to watch. The staff juggle schedules, even driving thirty miles farther when they heard of a dentist who definitely is able to accomplish more with Ben.

What about Camping and Overnight Fun?

Ben and his housemates have camped every year but one, when they chose to travel to a major league baseball game instead. They spent a night at a hotel then, taking rides on the People Mover and checking out the jazz and arts festival in Detroit the next day.

This past year, they spent two nights at the cabin owned by the mother of Ben's housemate, Orion. This picture is from those days. They prepared fun crafts and fun food with love and lots of laughter.

Pioneer Resources is another great organization in our area that—among many other things—provides an excellent camping experience which Ben has enjoyed for many years.

Orion and Ben have been classmates and housemates for twenty years as of 2018. Orion's mom, Joyce, is in their home at least once every week, and usually more than that. Ben doesn't allow me to be around much without consequences to staff, so I am grateful Joyce and Orion are there. We're so grateful they can share life together!

How Do I Know What's Going on When I'm Not There?

It took some time for me to develop confidence in the staff, though I was encouraged to call or stop in when I had questions or concerns. I receive many warm assurances now of the staff's affection for Ben. Some come in the form of text messages—especially from Kelly—including pictures of Ben at a special outing or playing with puppies at the local animal shelter. One was a happy face messaged from a bowling event. Sometimes it's just Ben, smiling for Snapchat fun! I hope to post more of them on this book's website.

What about Special Diets or Needs?

Ben must have specially prepared food; his team makes it palatable and consistent. I have picked up Ben on occasion and wished I could stay for supper when I caught the aroma of what they were serving! From the beginning of 2017, because of staff intentionality—and it took a lot of that and a lot of ingenuity to redirect Ben—he has lost over *sixty pounds* as of this writing. That was not an easy feat for a man who loves food more than about anything, but it was critical to his well-being!

Communication?

Everyone who works in Ben's home has learned Ben's personal sign language and gestures, helping Ben communicate his wants and needs. They support him through his bipolar outbursts and are trained to use Gentle Touch therapy in response to his fits. The staff prioritizes personal program goals for each man, fitting him into home life for continued emotional, spiritual, mental, and physical health.

Recently, Ben's sister Rachel was concerned when I mentioned that Ben was walking very hesitantly. Immediately his supervisor put an exercise program in place to monitor the amount of walking Ben is getting and to increase it, knowing that his braces can help him feel secure, but that he has to be challenged to get out of his chair after a long winter. Most recently, Ben was given a physical therapy evaluation. He now has an extra tall walker to use when he feels insecure, especially in the mornings when he wakes up. We hope that will help reduce the number of falls he suffers.

Will Your Loved One Be Treated with Dignity?

I did not believe anyone except family would be able to understand Ben's needs. Most of his communication is accomplished through a loose form of signing and gesturing to get his point across. Ben's home has hired people of quality and longevity, who respect and come to love the individuals they serve. I have heard them confirm that they truly understand what Ben needs most of the time. That has helped me relax.

One time, when Ben's home still housed six men, Eric told me he never took all six into the community at once, out of respect for them. He would never let them become a spectacle. He treated them with dignity. I can think of one time when that was not the case, and it had immediate ramifications for that staff person. (She is no longer there.)

Under Ben's current supervisor, Janessa, I fully trust they'll only take Ben to places where it's safe for him, and where he is comfortable. That kind of care and respect has earned my trust.

Also, I have been at every yearly planning meeting. I communicate in between. I take Ben to our home or to family gatherings twice a month. I make sure that goals are followed and that Ben's voice is heard!

A House, Yes. But, Family?

Seeing their relaxed photos framed on the walls of that beautiful home reminds me that Ben is an adult now; he has his home, his work, and his life to live. Witnessing camaraderie, "sibling rivalries," and tender moments between staff and the men is a confirmation that yes, he has *family* there too.

I hope you find answers to the difficult questions you have regarding your loved one. There are people and organizations who want to help you—maybe even people in your church or your social circle. Keep knocking on doors until you find answers. I will be posting organizations and suggestions from my readers on my websiteb also. And I will look forward to meeting you there, or at a local book store or speaking event.

What I know of the choices we made for our Ben is that placement in adult foster care was the right and very best move for Ben—and for us. Thanks to the people who work hard, living out the philosophy of freedom and dignity for our son, my husband and I and our other children are gratefully living our own lives as well. God bless all those who work for the betterment of people with varying levels of disabilities and *super* abilities.

CHAPTER 28

Love Is on the Move

Love will always find you!

Ben moved into a beautiful new home a few years after I wrote this chapter. It is full of conveniences for the men and for their team. It is every bit as beautiful as the best home in the newest neighborhood.

Ben has wonderful opportunities, yet his life bears no resemblance to our original dreams for him. His life is better than I thought it would be when we began the bipolar journey. He has a fabulous house manager who works tirelessly to ensure the four men living in their home have conscientious, caring staff. Yet when we think about or plan for Ben's future—the years he may well live beyond Ed or I—fear does grip our hearts at times.

That sweet, comical, two- to four-year-old brain makes everyone giggle, and his wisdom sometimes astounds us. There's an effervescent, childishly joyful spirit, too immature for guile or pretense. Women get an endearing kiss to the hand from Ben, quicker than many men would open a door for them. His curly-handed wave to a stranger from the car window earns a few embarrassed looks from people more accustomed to distance.

The horror of what can transpire when that same brain takes a bipolar plunge is mind-boggling. Early one spring day, I called Ben's manager, praying for a good report, trying to get my head around the night I'm about to describe. "How is he doing now? Any better?" I asked.

He responded that Ben was focused on the family. "In fact, he greeted me this morning," he said, "with 'Muhmuh, muhmuh,' question marks."

I commented on how tortured Ben is and wondered aloud when it would end. Always the realist, the manager's quick reply was, "*Never*. It will not change for Ben."

My mind zipped back to the gavel in the judge's hand upon Ben's eighteenth birthday and our appointment as his legal guardians. The judge had accepted the words of the professional representing Ben: "No, your honor, his mental ability will remain between two to four years of age. That will not change."

That's Ben's reality. *Our* reality. Orson Welles evidently said, "If you want a happy ending, that depends, of course, on where you stop your story." (https://www.goodreads.com/quotes/139273-if-you-want-a-happy-ending-that-depends-of-course) This book was *almost* complete—for many years. I just never felt like it had that happy ending. At least not the happily-ever-after type. I knew as I began this chapter on a Maundy Thursday, precisely thirty years after Benjamin's birth, that his incredible story and mine had to be finished. The characters that Ben drew called out to me to finish the book!

Some may know my younger sister, Ruth, and her husband Herb Boven. They own a beautiful, internationally acclaimed bed and breakfast resort called *Castle in the Country*. She knows about hard work and pursuing hopes and aspirations! (https://www.castleinthecountry.com)

I made a promise to her, on one of the darkest days surrounding Ben's twenty-first birthday, stubbornly stating that the book would not be complete until I saw hope on *every* page. I admit now that was a lofty commitment! Are there hopeful parts? Yes. Are there unusual God sightings? Yes. Are there lots and lots of happy times? Yes. But is there hope on every page? I'm not so sure.

On the way home on the night I'm remembering now, the night I was discussing with the house manager, I sat in stunned disbelief. Ben had visited our house. There were lots of laughs. We had a lovely dinner together and played for a while. He spent an hour being hugged by his dad, and fell asleep on my shoulder while watching a movie. There was lots of attention from his siblings too. It had all the ingredients of a great home visit.

I didn't give Ben the sedative sent home with him, because he *seemed* okay and even signed a request to go back to his house. I was gullible again. I pulled Ben away from a houseful of family—Ben, with severe attachment disorder? Not a smart move, especially without medication.

When we entered his driveway, Ben immediately tensed, noticing a strange car parked in front. One of two aides came out to warn us there was *behavior* in the house. We entered warily, and Ben's eyes glazed over immediately. He grabbed my arm. He stopped short of hurting me, but—as fast as a lightning bolt—shoved his favorite aide from the back.

Ed intervened then, to keep Ben from hurting anyone else. Ed held him off to the side, gripping his arms with both hands. It required all of Ed's strength for over ten minutes. Instinctively, I put a dining room chair between them and the rest of us. An unfamiliar aide—short, with warm eyes, and an attitude of organizational know-how—came from the back room, apparently leaving the housemate with the behavior issues there.

Quietly working, she put Ben's sedative and evening medications in a small bowl of applesauce and confidently stepped into his space. Smiling her calm, pleasant strength, she urged him into bending his tall frame over to accept the spoonfuls she was offering. His teeth were gnashing, clamping down on the metal spoon each time. He squealed, screamed, and squawked out his misery. She fearlessly and purposefully moved straight into his brokenness.

Ben gave the scream-like cry we were all too familiar with, not swallowing, kicking at her with his black tennis-shoed feet. With her in-charge smile, she persistently, gently moved toward him, instructing, "Ben, swallow. Ben, take a swallow. You'll feel better."

Finally, he swallowed and tore away from Ed, his oversize frame clumsily escaping out the front door, as if daring us to … to what? He stuck out his tongue while snapping his index finger and thumb together—his version of flipping us off. His two-year-old defiance glared out of his twenty-eight-year-old face. Ed and I sat down at the dining room table, trying to look disinterested at his silly antics outside the window.

After a few minutes, I moved surreptitiously to the farthest corner of the dining room. I kept my distance from the other man who was having issues, when he walked to the bathroom and came back to the kitchen. Finally, Ben entered again, acting repentant. Ed received a penitent hug.

But suddenly Ben lunged toward that housemate, who was now calmly getting a snack in the kitchen, giving him an angry push from behind. That movement threw his housemate onto the floor. This, of course, led to a renewed eruption of rage. The nameless employee was immediately on the floor, holding Ben's housemate down, keeping him from lunging back at Ben. Her body took the anger as she held him safe in her lockdown. Her calm spoke volumes to my pounding heart.

Ed knew Ben was totally exhausted at this point, and just needed steady direction. He grabbed Ben's favorite pajamas from the counter: the cartoon Halloween set that typically made Ben squeal with delight. Then he convinced Ben to follow him to his bedroom. Ed is never afraid for himself. I worry for his safety, but he laughs that off, saying he can always outsmart Ben. He's usually right, of course!

More screeching came from Ben as I headed to the car, so sorry I hadn't given Ben the sedative, and for Ben's misery in general. Knowing the staff went through this with anyone of the men at different times didn't make me feel any better.

I would find out later it was more of a comical scene in the bedroom than anything else. But there was no way of knowing that then.

On the way back to our home, a heavy silence filled the seat where Ben had sat almost two hours before. Ed's scratched hands gripped the steering wheel. Then a favorite song spoke into our wordlessness.

The bass pulsed through as the strings, other instruments, and voices rose in multiple layers, accompanying the powerful chorus. Slowly, the words of the song registered in my soul: "Love is on the move … Love is on its way, and it will find you." It was a song by Leeland, a Christian band that's been around since 2000. The song began to speak peace into my soul. "*It will, Ben! Love* will *always find you!* I agreed silently. (https://leelandonline.com/albums/love-is-on-the-move/)

At that moment I *knew* I had found the finish to this book—the conclusion for which I'd been waiting. This truth is what Ben's life has taught me so often: *God is faithful*. All around and through Ben's life, there is love—big, protective, and complete. God's love will always find me, and it will always find Ben!

This book is not just about our Ben and his brokenness, or his heart. It is not just about our family and its grief and triumphs. I genuinely believe this book is the human story of how desperately we *all* ache for love to find us!

This path of suffering with Ben has truly been a winding, difficult path. It has made Ed and I (and probably Ben's siblings too) hesitate and question everything we know about God. All of us have paths that lead to questions and make us wonder. A great scenario, of course, is for that examination to point us toward the Giver of hope and light, Jesus Christ. I pray this book leads you even one step closer to that place of acceptance.

Before Ed left Ben's room, he had reminded him, "Jesus loves you, Ben." The same quiet woman who had moved into Ben's mania earlier entered about then, and Ed heard her ask, "Ben, do you want me to pray a bedtime prayer with you?" Later, we found out she had been called to fill in for someone that evening. She almost never worked at Ben's home.

God was *definitely* on the move through hands, prayers, and actions of people all around Ben. I distinctly remember moving away from Ben and his housemate—protecting myself. Ed and that unselfish aide, on the other hand, were busy running *toward* Ben, as so many people in Ben's life have done and still do, on a daily basis.

This book is a story of God's love around Ben and around all of us. We don't always see it. God's love is not always sought or even wanted. But love is still on the move, and *that* is why I know that hope wins!

I hope this last charmingly energetic character will encourage a smile today. I am praying that love will find you and your loved ones, wherever you are!

FREE!

It doesn't matter how many times Ben has seen a butterfly.
His response is always the same.
Seduced by their filmy, gossamer wings, he flails his arms,
letting out a high-pitched squeal: "Muh, Dah!"
Running, pointing, he tries to catch it. Every time. Enthralled by their beauty.

Someday Ben's new body will emerge. He will be free from wounded brain and things
that make him insecure. He'll emerge from his cocoon
Totally free!
The essence of him will be there, the truest part of Ben, but
Free
to live in ways his caterpillar body never can.
We think of our first conversation with Ben then. So many things we want to say.
Conversations we've longed to have.
Then I wonder, *Will we even talk when we get there?*

Maybe the language of heaven is more like what Ben already possesses:
Unpretentious smiles. Unguarded affection. Unending wonder.
Unquenchable excitement for everything beautiful …
and for the Beautiful One.
Imagine!
God's whole big family, worshipping in spirit and truth, *free* from constraints of language!

TRIBUTE

I have talked about Eric—Ben's home supervisor—quite extensively in Chapter 23: PCP Time. Eric had life-threatening medical issues that forced him into early retirement after twenty plus years as a house manager with the MOKA organization, just months before his men moved into the beautiful new home provided by the MOKA Foundation, and pictured in Chapter 27: "Questions You Might Have". Eric had dreamed of and we had talked about that home for years. Instead, he watched others take his well-deserved place and move his men into their new home.

More than a year later, I planned a lunch where Ben could see Eric again. I couldn't tell Ben in advance, but I did once we were in the car. Ben was ecstatic that we were going to see Eric. He searched the restaurant and yelled a loud "Hahee!" several times as he brushed aside waitresses and customers, forcing his way to his friend. The whole luncheon was filled with Ben kissing Eric's face, stealing from Eric's plate, and putting his arm around Eric's shoulder.

I thanked Eric again for the respect, care, and love he had exhibited to Ben and I apologized that Ben had behaved poorly one of the last times they'd been together. (Which was part of the reason their parting lasted over a year.) I reminded Eric how important the "gentle teaching" was for all of Ben's staff as well. (https://gentleteaching.com) He had helped cement that in MOKA training. Eric then repeated something I've often heard him say in different words throughout the many years and many meetings we've shared with my boy.

"Each day when I walked in the door," he said, "I forgave the future. The past, for sure, but I also forgave the future."

It silenced me to hear the sentiment voiced in those words. I had harbored nervousness just hours before when I thought about Ben seeing Eric after so long. I contemplated with some anxiety, taking Ben into a busy restaurant and then back to his home, on my own. Eric's philosophy reminded me what real love looks like.

Two months to the day after that unforgettable lunch, Eric died very suddenly. I can't explain this to Ben. Every time he sees a picture of Eric, he signs "here," asking to see him. Thankfully, because Eric was a believer in Christ, I know he is celebrating in heaven right now, enjoying his reward. It's why I know Ben **will** see him again. I think these words of his are the best tribute I could ever give him. And, possibly, the best gift I can pass on to my readers.

"Each day, when I walked in the door, I forgave the future. The past, for sure, but I also forgave the future."

Eric Rettig
March 30, 1962 – December 27, 2017

friend

ABOUT THE AUTHOR

A winner of Guideposts Writers Workshop, Shar uses the artistic sketches of their nonverbal son, Ben, to reveal his silent life of global encephalopathy and mood disorders. Through experiences in assessments, medications, behavioral plans, therapies, and Adult Foster Care, she hopes to bring personal light to a complicated subject. Shar is a Mom of five adult children, two grandchildren and wife of over forty years to Ed,

As a worship leader for Focus on the Family events around the country, she used breakout sessions for moms of special needs families to learn what those disabilities meant for their marriages and families. This book was written, in part, to encourage families who have, or will, experienced a life-altering diagnosis. She also hopes to encourage churches and individuals to come alongside families and individuals that are struggling with mental health disorders, and all forms of disabilities. One great desire is to put this into the hands of young and older people who seek a rewarding vocation.

Shar loves meeting readers and friends at book signings and events around the country. Shar enjoys speaking, and singing at special events, worship services, and women's groups. Contact her at SilentAspirations.com

For fun, she teaches piano and voice to children and adults, in a private music studio in Spring Lake, Michigan!

Grandma with Kelvin, Jr.,
Grandpa with Ana;
enjoying life… and blueberries!

Printed in the United States
By Bookmasters